PRAISE FOR *OPEN*

"I like Craig Gross because he keeps it real—no fake shallow stuff with him. He has a deep passion to see people experience freedom, and in *Open*, he will help you find the freedom you've been searching for."

—Derwin L. Gray, lead pastor, Transformation Church; author, *Limitless Life*

"*Open* is one of the most relative and practical books on accountability I've ever read. Craig takes many routes, through stories from pop culture and his personal journey to help lead you to a life that's *open*."

—Josh McCown, NFL journeyman

"Craig Gross occupies a very, very important space in the Christian community and the culture at large. He calls men and women to not just fight addictive problems but gives them the tools, encouragement and community they need to actually get free and live free. But living free requires being *open* with your life, and Craig's incredible book is both a clarion call to always live in the light and simple instruction guide for how to ensure you stay there."

—Shaunti Feldhahn, social researcher; best-selling author, *For Women Only* and *For Men Only*

"Craig has been a friend and ministry partner for years. He has always been as helpful and hopeful as he is honest. This book comes to you in that spirit."

—Ryan Meeks, founding pastor, EastLake Church

"I don't say this often, but this book is a must-read. Every time I speak somewhere or get emails with people asking me how to find healing in particular areas, my response is always *community*. Craig does a beautiful job in articulating how the path to true joy is found in being real, honest, and accountable."

—Jefferson Bethke, author, *Jesus > Religion*

"This book will challenge you. And with good reason, because isn't that inherent to accountability? In a culture that grows increasingly autonomous, it is essential that we pursue one another with intentionality. From a man that has been blessed by the ministry of XXXChurch and the Gross family, I am thankful for Craig—his heart for and devotion to life lived together. I pray that this book will serve as a practical guide for openness and intimacy that reflects the communal nature of our Creator."

—Levi (the Poet) Macallister, spoken word and performance artist

"In a time when many of us communicate through quick, abbreviated texts, and social media lends itself to the proclamation of 'truth' through a series of monologues, Craig Gross reminds us that life is about authentic relationships; relationships that seek truth through *true accountability*!"

—Michael Guido, road pastor, PR Ministries

"*Open* by Craig Gross gives us a simple yet fresh look at what it really takes to overcome the many things that can consume us and can keep us from experiencing sustainable freedom through Christ and community. This book is a true road map to living life openly, honestly and with genuine courage."

—Judah Smith, pastor, City Church; *New York Times* best-selling author, *Jesus Is_____*

Open

WHAT HAPPENS WHEN YOU GET REAL,
GET HONEST, AND GET ACCOUNTABLE

CRAIG GROSS
with ADAM PALMER

THOMAS NELSON
Since 1798

NASHVILLE   DALLAS   MEXICO CITY   RIO DE JANEIRO

Published in Nashville, Tennessee, by Thomas Nelson. Thomas Nelson is a registered trademark of Thomas Nelson, Inc.

Published in association with the literary agency of Fedd & Company, Inc., PO Box 341973, Austin, TX 78734.

Thomas Nelson, Inc. titles may be purchased in bulk for educational, business, fund-raising, or sales promotional use. For information, please e-mail SpecialMarkets@ThomasNelson.com.

Names and identifying details of some people mentioned in this book have been changed to protect their privacy.

The websites recommended in this book are intended as resources for the reader. These websites are not intended in any way to be or to imply an endorsement on behalf of Thomas Nelson, nor does the publisher vouch for their content for the life of this book.

Library of Congress Cataloging-in-Publication Data

Gross, Craig, 1975–
  Open : what happens when you get real, get honest, and get accountable / Craig Gross, with Adam Palmer.
    pages cm
  Includes bibliographical references.
  ISBN 978-1-4002-0530-1
  1. Integrity—Religious aspects—Christianity. 2. Responsibility—Religious aspects—Christianity. 3. Honesty. I. Title.
  BV4647.I55G76 2013
  241'.4—dc23

Printed in the United States of America

13 14 15 16 17 RRD 6 5 4 3 2 1

Dad,

I know this past year has been tough on you and your health. I hope and pray you are the first one who is able to read the finished copy of this book. The last few years are ones I will never forget and always hold on to. A phone call you made to me over six years ago changed my life and will change our families' future for years to come. Thank you for everything you have done and provided. I look forward to watching another Super Bowl with you!

CONTENTS

If you want to go fast, go alone; if you want to go far, go together.

—African proverb

FOREWORD

*I*t's fitting that my friend Craig would write a book called *Open*.

My friendship with him began in the summer of 2006. I had simply reached out with some questions about starting a nonprofit, and he ended up offering me a surprising invitation to come live with his family in their basement in Michigan. Craig added that he would be traveling to speak at a bunch of churches and schools during that time, but that I should come with him on those trips as well.

His life was open. And I was invited in.

At the time, I had just quit my job in order to focus on

starting an organization to help people struggling with depression, addiction, self-injury, and suicide. The organization was born from the surprising response to a story I had written called "To Write Love on Her Arms," about the pain and hope of my friend Renee. We started selling T-shirts as a way to pay for her drug treatment, and the story and the T-shirts began to make their way around the world. The issues I had written about seemed to be issues a lot of people were living with, but they also seemed to be things that very few people were talking about.

Craig seemed to be doing a similar work helping people who were caught up in pornography, breaking the silence and offering hope and recovery in a world mostly secret.

So I made my way from Orlando to Grand Rapids, knowing very little about basements, the season of Fall, or what it might look like to run a non-profit. During the four weeks that followed, I must have asked Craig a thousand questions. And he didn't just answer the easy ones. He talked about the hard stuff too, the stuff that was tough within his job and within his life. And Craig had questions for me as well, about what made me tick and where I hoped to go with TWLOHA.

Our time together led to TWLOHA launching under the umbrella of Fireproof Ministries, which Craig leads and which XXXChurch falls under as well. It gave us a big brother we could go to with questions, someone to offer guidance and support and to help keep us accountable.

Over the last six years, we've been on our own as a non-profit, but Craig and I are still great friends. He is still someone

I look up to and lean on with questions. We still swap stories and share struggles and celebrate each other's victories. When TWLOHA won the $1,000,000 grant at the first-ever American Giving Awards in 2011, Craig was standing with me on stage. And while I am a huge fan of his work and how he goes about it, I am even more impressed by who he is as a husband, a father, and a friend.

Craig and I, along with our teams and our supporters, have learned that people all over the world can relate to pain, to questions, and to struggle. We've also learned that so many people feel alone and live alone when it comes to these things. It seems we're afraid of being labeled, afraid of being judged, misunderstood, abandoned. And it's easy to buy the lie that suggests our friends have enough on their plates—they have problems of their own and they don't need ours on top of them.

But the truth is that people need other people, that a good story requires more than one character. We were all made to be loved and made to be known, to find ourselves in honest relationships where those things can be reciprocated and exchanged. It's one thing to have hundreds of friends on Facebook or a phone overflowing with contacts. It's another to really let a few people know you, to have some friends who meet you in your questions, in your pain, and in your coping. We all deserve it—a community, a support system. It isn't easy, but it's worth it; for you were never meant to fake it or to hide. You were never meant to live this life alone.

Once again, my friend Craig is talking about some things that people tend not to. And he isn't just talking about this stuff, or saying that we need to talk about it. He's showing the way forward. And like the thousands of stories and pieces of stories I've had the privilege of hearing in recent years, Craig is not suggesting that any of this will be easy. But I believe he's saying that it will be worth it. Friendship is this incredible miracle gift that says we don't have to carry everything ourselves.

In Florida, we're afraid of basements because we imagine that they're ugly. We assume they must be dark and dirty and full of things from the past. Mostly, we're afraid because it's a place we've never been. I hope your experience with this book is like my experience with Craig and that basement in Grand Rapids. It's a different sort of life, and it's one we have to choose. It will involve some phone calls and surprising invitations. It will mean leaving your comfort zone and it may require airplanes. It will take some showing up and some letting people in.

I hope you're pleasantly surprised.

Jamie Tworkowski
Founder, To Write Love on Her Arms
April 24, 2013, New York City

GETTING OPEN

*A*ren't you Craig Gross?" the man next to me on the airplane asked.

"Yes," I replied.

"You're the x3Watch guy!"

"Yep."

We were on a flight from Las Vegas.

Now, Las Vegas bills itself as the Entertainment Capital of the World. Packed with casinos, bars, strip clubs, as well as the availability of legal prostitution less than sixty miles away, Las Vegas is a type of mecca for people who want to "have a little fun." I don't consider much of what Las Vegas has to offer as my type of fun, but a lot of people seem to feel that indulging in outlandish behavior and losing far more dollars than they win are "fun." After all, as the city famously declared in the early 2000s, "What happens in Vegas, stays in Vegas."

Since I do many speaking engagements, I travel a lot, which means I often find myself on planes flying to and from Vegas. When I lived in Vegas, I often sat next to people who had visited with the hope that the city would live up to its famous catchphrase (though it seldom did). Usually I wound up sitting next to someone who was heading home after a Vegas vacation, winging away from a pile of crazy acts he or she planned not to bring back home.

Which brings me back to the man in his twenties who happened to be sitting next to me and did a double take as he took his seat and adjusted his seat belt. He had recognized me from x3Watch.

What Is XXXchurch?

Let me pause for a moment to explain what the young man was talking about.

Back in 2002, I founded a website called XXXchurch.com. The point of this site was to address the repercussions of pornography—both in the people who used porn and became addicted to it, and in the people who made it. We wanted to offer help to anyone who had become enslaved to the pornography machine, whether they were in the industry and wanted to get out or were end users and wanted to clear it out of their lives.

Shortly after we started, and with those end users in mind, one of the ways we offered help was through an accountability software we called x3Watch. This is a program you download onto your computer or smartphone or Internet-enabled music player that keeps track of your Internet history, flags anything that looks suspicious, and e-mails a report to one or two people you trust. Since its introduction, x3Watch has become a major help to people who don't trust themselves to browse the Internet with integrity and who want support in staying away from the ever-lurking specter of porn.

Apparently my new airplane friend was a fan. At least I assumed so when he called out to another man a few rows ahead of us, "Hey! Craig Gross is back here! The x3Watch guy!"

Then he turned back to me. "That's my cousin. We both use your software. We're porn-free!"

"Great," I said, smiling enthusiastically. I always enjoy meeting people who've been helped by XXXchurch. "Glad it's helping," I said. While he nodded vigorously, I gestured toward his carry-on bag. "What were you guys up to in Las Vegas?"

He gave a coarse laugh, and his eyes went mischievous. "We were up to no good, man! Just spent the weekend hitting up the casinos and strip clubs!"

My smile went from authentic to worried. I don't think this man was aware of the bucket of irony he'd just put his foot into.

"You use x3Watch?" I said.

"Yeah, man!"

"So who's your accountability partner?" I asked.

"Just a buddy of mine."

"Does he know you came to Vegas? Does he know you and your cousin came out here to live it up like you did?"

He let out a matter-of-fact snort. "No," he said in a tone that indicated he thought I'd asked a ridiculous question. "We don't talk about that stuff."

A Peek into x3Watch

x3Watch exists because I sometimes let my mouth run ahead of my brain. In late 2001, I spoke at a pastors' conference about XXXchurch.com—a site that hadn't even been invented yet. We had stickers, some T-shirts, and a few blow-up dolls (to this day I still don't know why we had blow-up dolls), but we had no website.

Nevertheless, as I talked to more and more of the conference attendees, I managed to convince them that the site was going to be amazing. I even convinced myself! And then, to sweeten the deal, I told them that one day we would have free software that would help keep people accountable online.

People loved it.

We did manage to launch the website, and it was a big hit and still remains one to this day, blending the seedy with the sacred and helping people on both sides of the porn industry find freedom. But when it came to the accountability software,

I wasn't sure exactly how to make it happen. In fact, I naively thought we could just tell people the software was tracking their moves and that knowledge alone would keep them honest. I figured the very thought of having someone else see where you went online would work.

Of course, that isn't the case; so we decided we needed accountability software that actually worked as advertised. Unfortunately, we didn't have much money, so I had to find someone who could make a good product with the monetary equivalent of a matchstick, a paper clip, some duct tape, and a Magic Marker.

Enter Chris Huff. I met this programming genius through a mutual friend and told him our vision. He assured me he could design the software at minimal cost. A few months and a roll of nickels later (okay, maybe we paid him with a roll of quarters and a signed photo of actor LeVar Burton), he followed through and we had x3Watch.

This was huge.

This was a game-changer.

In total, as I write this sentence, x3Watch is in use on over one million computers and mobile devices, and that number grows daily.

Why?

Because when it comes to the Internet, there are many, many of us who want to be accountable.

So then, what do we do with my airplane seatmate? Here was a guy who was, quite literally, one in a million—he had downloaded x3Watch and was currently using it on his computer.

It wasn't some archaic thing he'd gotten awhile ago and never activated, nor was he some ironic hipster who laughed cynically at the concept. He was a believer in x3Watch; he actually thanked me for it during the course of our conversation; and after our flight was over, he introduced me to his cousin, who thanked me for it too. These weren't bad guys—they were just two men who recognized their need for accountability when they went online.

What they possibly failed to recognize, however, was their need for accountability everywhere else.

If they're trying to stay pure online, then why did they head to strip clubs while in Las Vegas?

And what about the casinos? Did either of them struggle with an addiction to the rush of gambling? Or were they about to form one?

And then there are the finances. Did these guys just get into a deep hole of soul-sucking debt simply for a chance to pull a couple of levers a few more times?

What did they eat while on their trip? Some people—a lot of people, actually—have a very hard time sticking to a healthy, balanced diet; and Las Vegas is a place of excess everywhere, not just on the sex and money fronts. Were these guys at risk for indulging in literally unhealthy appetites?

What about their relationships with their spouses, families, or friends? Did they need to be spending more time working on those instead of spending time on the Las Vegas strip?

Did they have any other unhealthy habits to discard, like tobacco use, alcohol, or harder drugs?

Why were they so keen on staying accountable in the online part of their lives but not in any of the other parts?

Now let me make one thing clear: I actually like Las Vegas. I like visiting there, and I liked living there. There is a lot about the city that is worthwhile, but it is the type of city that celebrates excess and wasteful living. Extravagance is a way of life there.

I don't think these guys were crazy for going to Las Vegas, but I do think they were crazy to go without telling anyone. They weren't telling anyone why they were going, where they were staying, or what their plans were while they were in town.

They were essentially going in secret—and when you start doing things in secret, you can start doing them to excess, and they can spiral out of control. That's when you have a problem.

They'd already dealt, or at least started to deal, with their porn problem by installing x3Watch on their computers. But there was a whole list of other possible problems they were walking right into, eyes wide open, with no one to get their backs.

Look, I'm not telling you all this as a commercial for x3Watch or to make myself feel important or famous. I'm telling you about these men because their compartmentalization of the different facets of their lives indicates a problem in our society . . . along with a deep desire.

That problem and that desire both have the same name: Accountability.

Time to Get Accountable

I strongly believe this world is filled with people who are seeking something broader, something deeper, something more intricate and complex. Our society has made it easier than ever to keep our relationships at a surface level—we can just click the "like" option on someone's Facebook status and then pat ourselves on the back for being "involved" in their life. We don't need to have a face-to-face conversation—we can just follow each other on Twitter. A simple tap and we just made an Instagram photo a "favorite," complete with an icon of a heart to represent our so-called love.

We are connected to more people than ever before, able to give and receive instantaneous updates on the minutiae of our lives . . . yet we remain curiously unsatisfied and isolated.

This life is meant to go far, far deeper than anything online. And while Internet accountability is a great thing (obviously I'm a champion of it), it's time to go further, deeper, and wider.

The time has come to carry accountability forward, to take it offline and into the real world. To share our lives with just a few people we really, truly, honestly trust.

My hope is that someday, someone—maybe even you—will sit next to me on a plane and start telling me how rewarding your life is now that you are accountable, living entirely free of secrets, walking in the self-confidence that comes from not having to look over your shoulder, worried about hidden flaws being discovered. That you are living a life full of grace extended and received, with stronger, healthier, and deeper relationships.

In the long run, that is what accountability is really about. It's about living a richer, more fulfilled, more satisfying life. Shelves and shelves of books have been written encouraging self-help, but the time has come to go beyond self-help.

It's time to get accountable.

It's time to get open.

Part 1

WHY

Why do we need accountability?
For every reason in the world . . .

Chapter 1

ACCOUNTABILITY IS GOOD

*I*t was a brisk morning in September 2011 when about a thousand people descended on Zuccotti Park in the Wall Street area of New York City. They came together to protest the ever-widening gap between who is considered rich and who is considered poor in the United States. Fed by the fires of social media and the general outrage of the average American, the gathering took on the name Occupy Wall Street and blazed into a full-on protest with thousands of participants.

If you want to know how the world feels about something, you turn to Twitter, where news breaks fast and where activist cries get picked up and repeated. At any given moment, the social media network sparks to life with quick-fire conversations about news as meaningful as the death of Osama bin Laden or as banal as the latest Justin Bieber video. Usually the most newsworthy items float to the top, however, and a movement like Occupy Wall Street was destined to do just that.

For those not familiar with the Twitterverse, one of the user-created functions is called the "hashtag." You create a hashtag by putting the hash mark (also known as the pound sign, "#") in front of a word or set of initials. Someone else sees the hashtag and starts using it. The more people who use a specific hashtag, the more popular the topic attached to that hashtag becomes.

The Occupy Wall Street protestors immediately began using the hashtag "#OWS," increasing the publicity of their movement and initiating a global response. Within a few weeks, similar protests began forming in cities across the United States and then across the world, and "#OWS" became one of the most popular hashtags on Twitter, being used once in about every five hundred hashtags. (For context, Twitter has about 175 million registered users, though many of those are people who don't necessarily make the most of the service.[1])

Now, whether you agree with the Occupy Wall Street movement or not, it is impossible to ignore that it became a worldwide symbol, a judgment on the rampant and unchecked greed in our financial system.

In other words, at its core, it was a call for accountability.

I'm just glad there was no Occupy Craig's Front Lawn in protest of all my misdeeds. But even if that ever happens, we should all be held accountable.

Held Accountable

With alarming frequency, we get news story after news story where someone in a position of power—say, some tyrannical dictator, toothy politician, or cynically underachieving CEO—abuses that power for his or her own good. And inevitably, as was the case with the Occupy Wall Street movement, the response is a clarion call from the media or from random people on the street that such a person be "held accountable" for the wrongdoing.

They oppressed or massacred thousands of people? They should be held accountable.

They bilked taxpayers out of millions of dollars? They should be held accountable.

They knowingly sold faulty mortgages destined for collapse in order to line their own pockets? They should be held accountable.

Obviously, such examples are legion, and in each case, I couldn't agree more—people who willfully hurt others for their own personal gain should be held accountable. That goes without saying.

But I suggest we take it further: we should all be held accountable.

Because accountability is a good thing.

Isn't Accountability a Little "Big Brother"?

I travel a lot talking about pornography, specifically Internet pornography, and the detrimental effects it has on people—both the people who use pornography and the people who make it. And because I talk about it a lot, I also wind up talking about the need for accountability on the Internet.

If you have a problem with—and by "problem with" I mean "insatiable, life-derailing thirst for"—pornography, one of the best ways you can help yourself manage that problem is by inviting someone else into it. Not to share the problem with you and get themselves addicted, but to keep tabs on you. As I mentioned in the introduction, a few years ago our ministry created free accountability software called x3Watch to help you do just that—you install it on your computer or your smartphone or your Internet-enabled music player and set it up so someone you trust, like your spouse or good friend (or both), can see a record of your online activity.[2]

The mere knowledge that someone else will be seeing where you go online—will be virtually looking over your shoulder as you browse the Internet—is a huge deterrent to leaping down the rabbit hole of porn. It just works.

But whenever I talk about Internet accountability, inevitably I run up against this charge: "Isn't that a little too 'Big Brother'?"

And it isn't just from regular opinionated Joes on the street either—I heard this phrase directly out of the mouth of none other than Dr. Phil himself. He had a couple on his show who uses x3Watch, and as they were describing it to him, he asked that exact question, invoking the terrifying term *Big Brother*. That phrase is on the lips of a lot of people who don't understand accountability—maybe even yours. Maybe you think, *Accountability? Isn't that a little "Big Brother"?*

You know what? In a lot of cases, the answer is yes.

What Is Accountability?

Before we go any further, we should probably push Pause for a moment and talk about what exactly I mean when I use the word *accountability*. There are a good number of possible definitions you could have in mind, so let's establish our definition while we're still in the early goings of this book.

When I say we all need to "get accountable," I mean we need to live our lives out in the open, simply and easily, with no fine print or legal jargon.

Perhaps you hear me tell you to get accountable and you think that just like corporate finances should have an overseer to help eliminate funny business or an out-of-control dictator is held in check by the United Nations Security Council, accountability provides you with an outside source of authority to help keep your life in line.

However, those are imperfect analogies, because those are more like policing people or installing a bunch of rules to follow.

That's not what I'm talking about.

We'll get into this more later, but the kind of accountability I mean isn't a police force or even a strict teacher who threatens to crack your knuckles with a ruler if you step out of line. What I'm talking about is a deep relationship, a support system.

Think about diving. Not like diving off a board and into a swimming pool, but diving into the ocean to explore. Now think about how far you can get if you just hold your breath. Even if you're a champion breath-holder, you can only give yourself a few minutes underwater before you have to come up for air. That means you have to stay pretty near the surface, doesn't it?

So on your own, you can't go very far.

Now think of accountability not as a policeman who tells you to get out of the water or as a boundary line that barricades where you can go, but as the scuba apparatus you wear on your back. It's the air you breathe underwater, allowing you to go farther and deeper and explore more than you ever would be able to on your own.

That's what I mean by accountability. It's a support system.

But all metaphors and analogies ultimately break down, and such is the case with this one. I don't want you to think of yourself as all alone down under the water, in the big, cold, lonely ocean, with no one around but a few schools of fish and the occasional life-threatening shark.

How about this? What if, instead of imagining yourself diving in the ocean with your own scuba gear strapped to your back, you picture yourself down there with a close friend, a relative, or your spouse? Now that you have that picture in your mind, imagine that the people diving with you are the ones with the air tanks strapped to their backs, and anytime you need a puff of air, they offer you their mouthpiece and let you breathe in that life-giving oxygen.

In other words, without that person or those people around you, you would drown.

That's accountability.

One more example, and this time I'll borrow a classic word picture about heaven and hell. The story goes that some fellow was given glimpses of the afterlife. The first stop was hell, where, instead of a lake of fire and poor souls being tormented by red underwear-clad demons with pitchforks, our observer saw a lush banquet table, full of delicious and appetizing foods of all kinds. It was a long, straight table, with chairs on either side, and seated in those chairs were all the people who'd been sent to hell. The obvious intent was that they were to eat their fill.

However, there was a catch. The food could only be eaten with the silverware provided—no hands or face-plants like you see in pie-eating contests at fairs. Ordinarily, this would not be a problem, right? Just pick up your knife and fork and go to town. Except the forks and knives and spoons all had extremely long handles, making it impossible for the banquet participants to feed themselves. Their arms were not long enough, and no matter how much they twisted and turned and contorted their necks and heads, they couldn't get the food into their mouths.

Anticipation quickly turned to frustration, and frustration was followed by anger as all these revelers in hell had to deal with squashed hopes and the realization that food and satisfaction would always be out of reach for them. Forever.

Then our observer was transported to heaven, and you know what he saw there?

The exact same setup.

Same table, same food, same chairs, same forks, same knives, same spoons.

Everything was the same, with one small, crucial, critical difference: everyone was feeding the person across from them.

Instead of being focused on themselves and finding frustration at the ends of their eating utensils, the people in heaven were focused on those around them and, in meeting the needs of others, found their own needs met. They were taking turns and taking care of one another.

When I talk about accountability, that's the mind-set I'm talking about.

What's Wrong with That?

Now that we're moving forward with a clearer idea of this concept of accountability, let me add a little bit to our previous discussion about accountability seeming to be like "Big Brother." I'll answer that question by asking another one: what, exactly, is wrong with letting someone else—someone you love and trust—know what you're doing and where you're going? I'm not talking about the kind of accountability that gets its own hashtag and is broadcast to the world, or the kind of accountability that is performed by some shadow government lurking in the dark corners of your web browser. I'm talking about letting in someone who has a vested interest in seeing you live the full, honest life you want to live. I'm talking about incorporating an accountability partner into your world to help keep you pointed in the right direction.

That's a great thing!

Accountability has nothing to do with exposing all your privacy to the entire world. In fact, it's the other way around. When you get accountable, you let just a few people into your personal world, and then you have the opportunity to be as open with everyone else as you care to be.

By the way, I hate to spoil this for you if you don't already know, but nothing you do on the Internet is private. Your computer's network card has a unique number assigned to it, your Internet connection has a unique address, and everything you do very well may be logged and cataloged by the company that provides your online access. If you visit a website, the owner of that website can find out your physical location, exactly what time you visited, how long you spent at the site, and all the different pages you went to on that site. If you clicked a link to get to their page, they know where that link was located, and if you clicked a link to leave their page, they know where you went.

Just so you know: plenty of people, almost all of them complete and total strangers, know what you're doing online. And if that's the case, what's wrong with opening up your online world a bit and letting a couple more people into the loop? Except these aren't anonymous people on the other side of your computer; these are people you know, love, and trust. How can that possibly be bad?

But this whole topic covers so much more territory than just the Internet and is about far, far more than pornography. That's a starting point, but it isn't the whole point. The whole point is this: if accountability works online, it will work even better in the real world.

Accountability isn't about embracing Big Brother—it's about seeking a holistic life, removing the boundaries of compartmentalization, and engaging every part of your lifestyle with every available part of the world around you. You may not struggle with pornography in the slightest, but I know you have some sort of weight that holds you down, something in your life you wish could be either removed or improved, and accountability will only assist you in that goal.

How does it help? You may be surprised.

My Road to Accountability

My own experience with accountability started in my teenage years, the summer after my sophomore year in high school, when my youth pastor, Tom, sought me out and asked me if I wanted to start meeting with him at McDonald's before school on Wednesdays. I initially balked at the six o'clock meeting time—any time before noon is early for an adolescent male—but after thinking it through I began to see how this could be beneficial for me and agreed.

See, as an outgoing, fun-loving fellow, I had plenty of friends at the time, but they were just pals and acquaintances, the types of guys I could talk about girls with or go see a movie with or just hang out with. Do all those normal teenage shenanigans with.

What I was lacking was a person I could really open up to. But not only that—I was also lacking the ability to open up. I didn't know how to do it or how to even go about doing it, and sometimes I didn't even know I needed to do it.

Then Tom came along with this opportunity to start meeting with him. I took him up on his offer, and not long after that, we started our weekly meetings under the golden arches. Finally, at long last, I had a person in my life I felt I could share real stuff with—stuff about my faith, about my doubts and fears, about my dreams for life and what those looked like. About the struggles and temptations I had as I stepped into adulthood, and how well or poorly I wrestled with those struggles and temptations.

Even better, though, was that I now had the opportunity to listen as Tom shared with me some of the challenges he had in his own life. Maybe it sounds weird, but I didn't feel like he was unloading on me or using me as an ear to vent into—he was just trusting me with a small part of his inner world, a part that I was old enough and mature enough to hear about. He was showing me the flip side of accountability—it's not all about talking; it's just as much about listening.

There I was, a teenage kid, awed and amazed at Tom's ability to listen to me as I poured out my heart and his willingness to share a little bit of his heart with me. I couldn't believe it. I had mistakenly thought adults had it all together. You can imagine the paradigm shift I underwent the first time I heard Tom talk about some of the challenges he faced in his own life. Here was a guy who had progressed much further in life than I had, who had his career and life plan figured out, and he still had struggles.

It was liberating.

From Accountability Partners to Group

Tom and I continued to meet together, one-on-one, through my entire junior year. The following summer, though, he suggested an addition, mentioning the possibility of bringing in my friend Jake and turning our weekly meeting into a full-fledged accountability group. Jake and I knew each other really well, and though we'd had some deep talks before, we'd never dived as deeply into each other's stuff as we probably should have or could have. But now we had a great opportunity to be intentional about just that—all our normal small talk and goofing around could come at another time; now we had a guaranteed hour, once a week, to get down to business.

Senior year began, and Tom started mentoring Jake and me in how to keep each other accountable. He taught us what accountability should look like. He taught us about treating each other's struggles with love, respect, and grace.

He taught us that accountability is not about sitting across from someone as a judge, but about sitting next to him as an advocate.

And you know what? It worked. Jake and I graduated and went on to college. We became roommates. We eventually got into ministry together. We met a couple of girls, fell in love with them, and then married them and started our own families.

Tom was in both our wedding parties.

And now, twenty years later, Jake and I are still doing this, still hanging out once a week (though now on the phone) and getting into each other's worlds. We've been at it for twenty years, and our lives have been irrevocably changed for the better because of it.

Accountability is not easy, and it doesn't come naturally. But in the long run it's incredibly necessary, and when you do it right, it's nothing but good.

The Benefits of Accountability

There are far more benefits to accountability than we can list here. But one of the greatest benefits that comes from being accountable is the ability to live a life unencumbered by many of the unnecessary weights we add to it.

We come into this world with nothing in the way of material things—just our own skin and internal organs and the factors of the environment we are born into. A mom and a dad, or just one of them, or none. Brothers and sisters, or just a brother and a sister, or just one of them, or none. A lot of money, or a middle-class upbringing, or extreme poverty.

You get the idea. There are many intangible factors that contribute to who we are and who we become. And as we get older and more mature, we tend to start adding things to our lives to help us deal with those contributing factors. Maybe you grew up without money, so you add an unhealthy pursuit of material wealth in adulthood. Or maybe the converse is true; maybe you grew up wanting for nothing, and as a result you have experienced a form of emptiness and have since rejected material wealth, adding simplicity to your worldview.

Sometimes we add these things because we think they'll make life better; sometimes we add them to cope with a current situation; sometimes we add them in order to make it through the day.

The problem is that we often add these things to our lives, learn to live with them, and then find ourselves at a point where we can't live without them, even if they are no longer healthy (or never were in the first place). The problem then becomes this: instead of contributing positively to life, all our little additions grow to the point where they become obstacles and weights that detract from life.

When you get accountable, you get to figure out which of these things you need and which ones you can get rid of. So let's take a quick look at some of the unnecessary weights that accountability lets you leave behind.

No Secrets

There are plenty of things in this world that you should keep secret—the PIN for your debit card, for example, or the guest list for your best friend's surprise birthday party—but if a secret is starting to destroy you from the inside out, it has stopped being worthwhile and has instead become a weight you need to get rid of through accountability.

Maybe you are trying to eat better but are finding it difficult to say no to those midnight runs to Taco Bell. Maybe you're spending more time at work playing online games than you are doing your actual job. Maybe you find yourself stopping by casinos that aren't on the way home. Maybe you just feel stagnant and need to get organized or learn something new to help you enjoy life more.

Jon Kitna is a former quarterback who played for many years in the National Football League and is also a friend who works with XXXchurch to help us get out our message of accountability. This guy is serious when it comes to staying accountable.

Jon started his NFL career with the Seattle Seahawks, spending three years in the Pacific Northwest before becoming a free agent and signing with the Cincinnati Bengals. He was a new guy in a new city in a new part of the country, with all of his old friends thousands of miles away. He had no support system and suddenly realized he had a major opportunity to live a secret lifestyle. Pornography, gluttony, habit-forming substances, even an adulterous relationship—all of them were within arm's reach, and all he had to do was take them.

No one would have to know.

This was not a road Jon wanted to go down, so he started seeking out someone to be accountable to. Eventually he crossed paths with another player on the team who was having the same struggles, and the two of them began leaning on each other to stay strong and to support each other. Their two-man group has now grown into a four-person group that keeps each member accountable and living a life free of secrets.

These guys take their accountability seriously, to the point where they talk with one another almost every day. "We don't meet once every two weeks," Jon says. "We do life together. If we don't hear from someone in the group for a couple of days, we all know something's up."

Here's how open Jon is with his group: though he is no longer in the NFL, he still travels quite a bit doing speaking engagements. When he goes on the road, Jon gives his accountability group his itinerary so they know what time he is scheduled to show up in his hotel room. As soon as he arrives, he uses his smartphone to take a video of himself disconnecting the adult channels from the television, then he e-mails that video to the other three members of his group. If they haven't received a video from him within an hour of the time he was supposed to have arrived at his hotel, they start sending text messages checking in on him.

"Without these guys," Jon says, "I would be failing. Left to myself, my thoughts are wretched."

Though Jon is an outspoken proponent of x3Watch and one of those million people who use it every time he goes online, he has taken his accountability much deeper than our software could ever go. He is a good example of someone using account-ability to enrich every facet of his life. And he isn't ashamed of his need for accountability; on the contrary, he flaunts it.

In fact, Jon doesn't call his group an "accountability" group. He says it is so strong and has had such a positive, life-changing effect on each of the guys in it that they refer to it as their "covenant group."

Jon, along with all the other men in their covenant group, knows what I know: accountability is good.

And as long as we're talking about the x3Watch software . . . while most of our users are very pleased with the way it works, some of them don't like the icon the mobile app has: a steel-gray box with a big "X3" stamped in the center of it and the word "watch" in smaller letters underneath.

"Craig," people say to me, "why does this thing have to have that big *X* on it? Why can't it be more discreet?"

To that I always say, "Why don't you want people to know that you're keeping yourself accountable?"

No matter what you're keeping yourself accountable for, you have to put yourself in the mind-set that this is a good thing. It's not that you're in trouble or that you're trying to keep yourself from doing something wrong. Instead, you're using every possible tool you have at your disposal to live a stronger, richer, more rewarding life.

When you keep secrets—even the secret that you're keeping yourself accountable—they eventually will eat at you until there's nothing left. By letting other people into your life and sharing those secrets with them, you get the horrible weight off your shoulders and out into the open, where you can start to find healing. Sometimes all you need to do to feel better is to let your secret out. Simply verbalizing a secret can be a tremendous relief from the stress of keeping it.

Organizations like Alcoholics Anonymous, Sexaholics Anonymous, and even Weight Watchers know this concept well, understanding that there is no benefit to absolute secrecy in the areas where you have struggles. Take Weight Watchers, for example: Is that organization seeing positive results because of the food and diet programs it offers, because of its point system to eating, or because of its encouragement to exercise?

Surely those things are contributing factors, but eating smarter and exercising is a no-brainer for people who seek to lose weight and keep it off. You can do those things on your own. Weight Watchers has succeeded in large part because of its emphasis on support and accountability. When you have accountability, you don't have secrets, and you are able to lose weight.

No Hiding

If you're keeping your actions a secret, then most likely you're doing more than just zipping your lip—you probably also have evidence you need to dispose of: a web browser history that needs to be cleared, a candy bar wrapper that needs to be thrust to the bottom of the trash can, a few dollars missing from the company's petty cash drawer that need an explanation.

One of the most prevalent examples of this type of behavior

can be seen online, and not just with pornography. Social media has opened up the world in many beneficial ways, but it also has removed barriers between us and our baser impulses. Now, if we're not feeling especially loved at home, unconditional acceptance is only a chat window away.

I'm talking about cheating.

More and more people are turning to social media sites like Facebook—especially Facebook—to pursue relationships outside the one they're in. From the casual fling to the high school hookup to torrid confessions of love in a Facebook message, people are using the connectivity of social sites to indulge their lusts and passions. In fact, the word *Facebook* is now cited in one out of every three divorces.[3]

Social media users are hiding their online lives.

I've seen story after story after story of jilted boyfriends or disillusioned wives who have discovered that the person they love has been carrying on a secret relationship through Facebook, Twitter, LinkedIn, Instagram, and plenty of other social media hubs, including some dating sites. In fact, our ministry now runs a website called FacebookCheating.com to help tell those stories as cautionary tales. With each one I read, I see that the discovery of an affair wrecks the discoverer emotionally, and often the person who has been cheating expresses an exhausted relief that he or she has been found out.

There are hundreds of stories on that site, and almost all of them feature the same sort of pattern: a spouse or significant other signs up for Facebook, often with the help of their committed partner, and things go fine for a little while before suddenly the spouse or significant other begins acting suspicious and starts hiding something. Maybe an old high school flame has sent a friend request, or maybe the new Facebook user is the one sending the request. The secrecy and hiding continue until the cheated-on spouse or significant other gets wise and does some detective work to uncover the truth of cheating.

In one of the stories on FacebookCheating.com, the cheating spouse simply began playing Words with Friends with random strangers and became so secretive that it aroused her husband's suspicions. Months later he found out she'd been meeting one of her Words with Friends partners for sex once a month, and she soon moved out to live with him.

So much hiding. So much deceit and suspicion.

Hiding your true behavior is no way to live. Cheating is reprehensible, and if you're struggling with it, you need to start seeing a professional counselor to get at the root causes of why. But if you're even struggling with thoughts of cheating or if you have an ulterior motive for sending that friend request to the attractive person from your past, you don't need to manage those thoughts and feelings on your own.

By getting accountable, you're discussing these things in the open with someone you trust, often discovering patterns or behaviors you didn't even know were there. What a joy to be able to let go of some of these load-bearing practices. We often don't deal with any of this stuff in our lives until there's been an affair or some transgression, but accountability gives us a platform not just to prevent the behavior or deal with the impulses for that behavior but to examine why we feel the way we do. To uncover why we might be seeking out other partners.

In this way, accountability can be preventative and squash potential missteps (or worse) right away. It can be a proactive means of living out in the open instead of a reactive life of secrets and hiding.

No Worry or Guilt

When you have secrets and hide behaviors, you live in a constant state of worry, a continual fear that you will be discovered. You're restless, always looking over your shoulder, waiting for the inevitable moment when you will be found out, whether it's in the next thirty seconds or thirty years from now. You can't relax and you can't enjoy life because of that gnawing, looming dread that all those secrets you work so hard to keep hidden will eventually bubble to the surface.

Your mind becomes a sounding chamber for worry. *Did I clear my browser history? Did I throw away that cheeseburger wrapper, or did I accidentally leave it in the car? I can't detect any smoke on my coat, but is that just because all those cigarettes have wrecked my sense of smell?*

We can get a dramatic, behind-the-scenes view of the widespread effects of worry and guilt in, of all places, William Shakespeare's masterpiece *Macbeth*. This time-honored play depicts the tragedy of a greedy husband and wife who murder their way to the throne of Scotland, only to be undone by their worry and guilt.

Now, I'm more of a TMZ guy than a classical literature

guy, but I can't ignore the parallels between this classic story and the types of secrets we all tend to keep if left to our own devices. In the play, Lady Macbeth convinces her husband to murder the existing king of Scotland and take over his throne. But once the deed is done, both husband and wife immediately begin to worry that their cunning will be discovered. They are terrified they will be found out, so they continue on their murderous path. The body count grows, eventually engulfing entire castles full of innocent people.

Lady Macbeth is the main mouthpiece for this worry and guilt; she is given a memorable moment in the play where she sleepwalks, dreaming of bloodstains on her hands that won't wash off (the immortal phrase "Out, damned spot!" comes from this scene). Eventually, Lady Macbeth is so plagued with remorse, worry, and guilt that she takes her own life in order to be at peace.

This is no way to live. And when you get accountable, you don't have to. There is no liberation quite like the feeling of being able to focus fully on the world around you without the constant, nagging distraction of making sure you've covered your tracks and then worrying about whether you've done it well enough to avoid detection. If you're living a life free of secrets, you'll never have to worry about being exposed. And that is a wonderful feeling.

No Isolation

The poet and priest John Donne famously wrote, "No man is an island," meaning that we, as human beings, cannot exist totally isolated from others. We crave relationship at a basic level. Yes, there are those who seek relationship more than others, and those who seek it less than others, and some of us are more extroverted while others are more introverted; but on the whole, we all want to have a little interaction from time to time with someone else.

But beyond surface-level, this-is-some-weather-we're-having kinds of conversations, I believe we each have an innate desire to share a life with someone else. Call it community, call it tribalism, call it what you want—we need others.

Here's the kicker, though: we don't just need to be heard; we also need to listen. That makes accountability perfect. It isn't a one-way arrangement where you get to unload all your stuff on someone else and let them do what they want with it. Instead, you also get to hear from them what kind of stuff they're dealing with, and you get to offer support to them in their difficulties.

When you get accountable, you get the opportunity to look someone in the eyes and tell them exactly what you've been up to. The good, the bad, the exciting, the bland . . . everything. And they tell you. You are sharing in the very act of living, and all the while you get to deepen your relationship with that person. When temptation comes, you aren't facing it alone—even if you're by yourself, you, in a sense, have your accountability partner with you. They're with you because you have the anticipation of how they'll feel when you inevitably tell them the way you reacted to that temptation, whether that's a story of gloriously deflecting it or regretfully embracing it. And you know they're going to be on your side, no matter what.

But there's more to it than that, because you also get the opportunity to have someone else look you in the eye and tell you what they've been up to. And for some people—certainly not you, right?—this can be a challenge. It can be difficult to be a good listener, the type of person who can sit with a sympathetic ear and a quiet tongue and allow someone to unload their troubles on them. Listening is definitely an art that must be cultivated in an accountability relationship, but one that is well worth doing. When you learn to listen without jumping in or judging, you are being the kind of listener you would want to talk to, and isn't that really the best for everyone involved?

With accountability, you listen and you're listened to. This is extremely empowering for both of you, adding to your self-worth and self-confidence and freeing you even further to live a fearless life.

Accountability in the Real World

Now that you've seen the benefits, let's move this out of the realm of the theoretical and take a moment to imagine how something like accountability can provide help in your specific situation, in your actual life. The benefits of accountability in the real world are practically limitless.

Career

No matter your job or how principled you are, there are always temptations to cut corners or shirk duties, especially if you don't have a manager or boss hovering over your shoulder at every moment to make sure you do everything just right. From small things like tacking ten extra minutes onto your lunch hour each day to big things like cooking the books, accountability and oversight go a long way.

Another one of the main areas where people in general feel a need to improve is organization. As a society, we tend to be a disorganized mess in some parts of our lives, and one of those parts tends to be the workplace. Accountability can help you nail down your world and get your stuff together and in order, with everything in its right place. How much would that help you during your workday?

Health

Maintaining a healthy lifestyle in our current culture is simultaneously one of the easiest and most difficult things to do. On one hand, a healthy meal is fairly easy to procure, and exercise is widely accepted as a wholesome, necessary thing. On the other hand, poor meal choices are even easier to find (and tend to cost less money), and unless you're one of those people who get a tremendous kick from endorphins, exercise is just hard. Being healthy is one of those things that we all seem to want to do, and we can even get started fairly easily—but maintaining a healthy lifestyle with any amount of longevity seems to be difficult.

Have you heard of CrossFit? This is a relatively new craze in personal fitness that has taken off like a rocket. But unlike a lot of exercise crazes that burn brightly for a moment and then flame out (can you say "NordicTrack"?), CrossFit seems to be here to stay. It has grown from the garages and warehouses of the world to a full-fledged movement with its own annual games and an official partnership with Reebok for an entire line of CrossFit-themed shoes. I make fun of my friends who wear the shoes, and they give me a hard time for quitting CrossFit after only two weeks.

Certainly part of the cachet of the program is that it is used by many police officers, military personnel, and elite athletes. There's a certain feeling you get using the same workout as exceptionally healthy people that makes you want to pat yourself on the back. Plus, the program's workouts are tough enough to be effective but varied enough to be engaging mentally. I've dabbled with CrossFit enough to know that it's pretty good (though I have a difficult time keeping up any kind of exercise regimen).

Aside from those features, one of the great benefits of CrossFit, and the main reason I think it's becoming so popular, is the program's emphasis on community and, as an offshoot of that, accountability. Most people who participate in the program do so with others, challenging and supporting and pushing one another to give their all to finish the workout of the day. There is a genuine sense of camaraderie around those who do these workouts, and that accountability has helped many a CrossFit athlete finish a particularly tough round of rope ascents or the hellacious up-and-down exercise they innocuously call "burpees."

But even if we're just trying to eat better or take more

walks, having someone keep us accountable can help us make health goals and stick with them, even when they become difficult to maintain.

Relationships

Want to be a better friend? A better coworker? A better family member?

Want to spend more time with your spouse or your kids but find yourself wasting it on stupid, inconsequential stuff? Believe it or not, accountability is a perfect way to help you in this area, providing real-world (but loving) consequences for the ways you waste your time or inject detrimental things into your various relationships. (By "detrimental things," I mean the selfishness and relational apathy that all of us struggle with from time to time.)

So, if you want to see advancement in *all* the relational areas of your life, you can start by getting accountable.

Marriage

Accountability will work wonders in any marriage because it allows a husband and wife to live at peace with each other, knowing that there are no secrets between them. It creates a marvelous sense of openness, in that there is nothing hindering you from loving your spouse to the fullest. In fact, I'd like to reclaim the phrase *open marriage* and redefine it. Instead of using it to label acknowledged cheating, I want it to describe the perfect kind of marriage—the kind built on accountability, honesty, and transparency.

You and your spouse don't necessarily need to be accountable with each other (though that in itself can be a wonderful experience—more on that later in the book), but the mere fact that you are seeking accountability with a trusted friend of the same gender adds immensely to the trust and peace that a marriage relationship requires.

Other Addictions or Struggles

While porn is the big one, accountability can help with any other addiction or even just a bad habit. Anywhere from gambling to overeating, from alcoholism to drug addiction—knowing that you will have to give an account for where you've been and what you've done helps you deter your behavior and make better choices.

Wherever you have struggles, be they internal or external, in your mind or in your body, there's a way to add some accountability and openness in order to help you move forward and gain traction.

Now that we've taken a broad-brush look at the benefits of accountability, let's start digging deeper into some of the specific outcomes we get when we get accountable. One of those key benefits to getting accountable is a tremendous feeling of safety. That's something we'll look at more deeply in the next chapter.

Chapter 2

ACCOUNTABILITY IS SAFETY

7 am a big, big fan of movies, and while my love for movies is large, it doesn't necessarily extend to every movie ever made. In some ways, I am a typical guy, tending more toward action-oriented films, though I do like many other critically acclaimed movies as well.

I guess what I'm trying to say is, I'm not a fan of *Titanic*.

I've seen it once and did not need to go see it again in 3-D. But when the 3-D version of the film was released recently, I started thinking about the events of that night and the way they relate to exactly what we're talking about in this book. So let's look back on that fateful evening—not the movie version, but the actual story—and see what lessons it holds about the necessity of accountability.

It was the dead of night, a chilly evening on the deck of a ship in the middle of the Atlantic Ocean. On April 14, 1912, at 11:40 p.m., a man named Frederick Fleet looked out from the deck of the RMS *Titanic* and saw everyone's worst fear: an iceberg. The crew reacted as quickly as they could, but the bulky cruise ship was hardly nimble; despite evasive maneuvers, the floating behemoth crashed into her icy nemesis, being greeted by holes punctured in her side and setting into motion one of the most well-known tragedies of the modern era.

But what made the sinking of the *Titanic* so tragic was not the hull breach itself or even the ship going down. No, it was the incomprehensible and completely unnecessary loss of life. There was a serious breakdown in the safety procedures, both in the number of lifeboats and in the number of people who eventually occupied them.

For starters, there were the lifeboats. Or, more accurately, the lack of them. An outdated quirk in the laws that governed oceangoing vessels at the time meant that the *Titanic* wasn't carrying enough lifeboats to handle all her passengers and crew. After all, why would you need something as wasteful and redundant as lifeboats on a ship that was considered unsinkable? Instead, the lifeboats could handle just about half of the total number of individuals, combining both passengers and crew.

So, you have this giant ship with enough lifeboats to carry only half of the people onboard. In addition to that hubristic oversight, the crew of the *Titanic* had not been trained properly on how to use the lifeboats and, as a result, were unsure how many people each boat could safely accommodate before the lifeboat itself sank. This led to the crew being overly cautious once the ramifications of the accident set in. When they started evacuating people, the crew unknowingly launched the lifeboats before they'd reached full capacity; some of the rescue vessels were filled only half full.

What an appalling lack of concern for safety. If only someone somewhere along the line had diagnosed the many safety pitfalls of the *Titanic* and done something about them, then perhaps they could have saved some—if not all—of the 1,514 lives that were lost on that fateful night.

Sadly, history is littered with stories of fail-safes ignored or not even put into place. If you're from America, the chances are good that I only have to say the words "Hurricane Katrina" and your mind automatically conjures images of breached levees, flooded city streets, and more unnecessary waste. If you know any of the story, you probably know that the levees that were intended to hold back the Gulf of Mexico from the coastal city of New Orleans, Louisiana, were insufficient—and had been so for years. A Katrina-like disaster was practically inevitable.

Or what if I say "Fukushima Daiichi" to you? You may immediately remember the horrific earthquake and subsequent tsunami that struck the coast of Japan in 2011, the enormous wave that swept away cars and buildings, the shuddering rock that disrupted nuclear reactors in the area and led to full meltdown. Yet again, a lack of safety measures and an enormous governmental overconfidence led to a deeper, more cataclysmic outcome.

In all the above examples, unstoppable outside forces (an iceberg, a hurricane, and a tsunami) caused a catastrophe, and in all three cases, safety measures were woefully inadequate to handle these seeming inevitabilities.

Secrets Exposed in the Secret Service

Then there's the idea, generally true, that even our most upstanding institutions are keeping us safe. We know we can mostly count on the police department, the fire department, and emergency medical personnel to take care of us in an emergency. Yes, there are bad apples in every organization, and no institution is immune to corruption, but surely we can trust the individual people who are supposed to protect us.

I'm sure, in the case of the Secret Service—the security detail in charge of protecting the financial systems in the United States, as well as the president of the United States— that's mostly the case, and I'm positive that an overwhelming majority of the people who serve in the Secret Service are fine, upstanding people. Perhaps that's what was so shocking about the scandal that came to light against the Secret Service in 2012.

While an advance team of Secret Service personnel were in Cartagena, Colombia, to protect President Barack Obama as he prepared to attend the sixth Summit of the Americas, several members of the team obtained the services of allegedly twenty prostitutes, bringing them back to their taxpayer-funded hotel rooms.

This odd behavior came to light after one of the agents agreed to terms with a prostitute named Dania Londono Suarez, the two of them settling on a fee of eight hundred dollars for an evening before the agent escorted Suarez to his room. The following morning, when she attempted to get the remainder of her fee, the agent simply refused and kicked her out of the room.

Suarez created a ruckus in the hallways of the hotel, arousing the attention of a couple of other agents, who did try to assist her, but to no avail. Eventually she took her tale to the police, and that's when the scandal came to light.

Of course, there was some concern that any of these prostitutes had unknowingly been given secret or sensitive information about the president's impending visit and itinerary, which would compromise his security and put him in danger.

But beyond those concerns were others about the character that had been exhibited by these Secret Service agents, behavior that prompted President Obama himself to deem them "knuckleheads."[1] Investigations ensued (and as of this writing are still underway), some of the agents were fired or resigned, and others were placed on administrative leave.

Perhaps the most comical aspect of the scandal was the imposition of new rules for Secret Service personnel. As a direct result of this incident in Cartagena, agents are restricted in who is allowed in their hotel rooms and are now prohibited from visiting "non-reputable establishments" while on assignment or from imbibing alcohol up to ten hours before starting work.[2]

I call this comical because it is so very backward. No amount of rules can change behavior if no one is around to enforce those rules. I'm reminded of the classic exchange from the sitcom *Seinfeld*, where perennial wheedler George Costanza is about to be fired from his new job because he engaged in sexual relations on the desk in his office with the after-hours cleaning lady. His new boss mentions this to George, who, trying to talk his way out of being fired, replies, "Was that wrong? I tell ya, I gotta plead ignorance on this one, because if anyone had said anything to me at all when I first started here that that sort of thing was frowned upon . . ."

There are some things we already know; we don't always need a new rule to be put in place in order to correct our behavior or keep us safe. In the case of these Secret Service agents, they acted the way they did because they'd done it before and not gotten in trouble. As a result of the Colombia scandal, a further investigation was done, which has uncovered a series of allegations—many of which are patently false, but some of which merit further consideration—stretching back to 2004.

Clearly, there was a lack of accountability for some members of the Secret Service. And as a result, safety was compromised.

But back to the examples I mentioned at the beginning of the chapter. What it comes down to is this: life is going to throw things like those icebergs, hurricanes, or tsunamis at us that we cannot anticipate or expect. Those are inevitabilities. But when disaster strikes, will we be prepared, or will we be overconfident in our abilities to withstand it, only to find out how inadequate our safety measures really are?

We Need to Stay Safe

I am a provocateur and a risk-taker. That's part of who I am and part of how I got where I am today. I am not the type of guy who's satisfied with waiting in the wings or playing it safe. I think feathers need to get ruffled and the status quo needs to be upset every now and then—that's how we achieve progress, and that's how we get messages across to those who long ago tuned us out.

So when I say that accountability is safety, don't think I'm advocating something I'm not. I'm not saying we all need to retreat into shells and refuse to interact with the world, refuse to say anything outlandish, refuse to speak our minds or lovingly provoke people. In fact, I think it's good to do those things in order to rouse the establishment out of complacency—that's why I do it so much.

But there's a reason I feel confident in the crazier things I say and do, and that reason is accountability. I have people in my life who have the liberty to keep me accountable, to hold my feet to the fire. They have that liberty because I've given it to them; I invited them into my world to help keep me safe. They keep me grounded and prevent me from coming unhinged; it's much easier—and more worthwhile—to provoke others to action when you're coming from a place of security and safety.

Here's how that started. You'll recall that I was already in an accountability relationship with my friend Jake, which started in high school. My wife and I have a great relationship as well, but a few summers ago, I was sitting on yet another plane, examining my schedule for the upcoming fall, and starting to feel a creeping panic and dread at all I had to do. This is a good problem to have, of course, but it's still a problem.

I was looking at all these speaking engagements, plus several meetings and other business- and ministry-related things that required my presence and input. In the meantime, I was trying to be a husband and a father who sows time into those relationships as well, and my kids weren't going to be spending any time that fall getting younger.

I was stuck. How would I get all my work done while still putting my family first?

I needed support.

I needed accountability.

The two are practically interchangeable. Think of accountability as a support system, or a foundation of sorts. When you're living a life free of secrets through accountability, when you have that bedrock safety, you feel an immense freedom to be wholly and completely yourself. And not just yourself, but the best version of yourself.

The stronger the foundation, the more solid and secure is

the building that sits on it. When you build your world on the platform of accountability, you get a lot stronger.

When I needed help to figure out how to manage my increasingly hectic schedule, I turned to accountability.

Some people tend to think of accountability as some sort of impersonal, always-watching police state. Not so! I'm not talking about turning over every aspect of your life to some impersonal, faceless corporation (though many of us already do that through social media like Facebook and Twitter) or letting some web-coding nerd tromp through your darkest secrets to pass on the juicy bits to his superiors.

The thing about accountability is that it's the exact opposite of those fears. This is far from faceless interaction or worry that your every move is being watched, your every mistake a looming threat to your security. This is, instead, an intimate, intentional, deep relationship with people you care about and who care about you. Rather than ramp up fears of being watched, accountability provides immense peace of mind, the type of worry-free living that comes with sharing your life with others and going deep with them.

We Want to Share

I just wrote that we tend to share even the most mundane parts of our lives through social media, and though that is a subject that could cover an entire book by itself, the concept does make sense when we're talking about accountability.

There's something to this, some reason we feel the need to update even our most mundane moments ("just woke up; gonna eat breakfast") or upload a picture of our latest meal ("peanut butter smoothie first thing in the morning") or barf out our current emotional state ("bad smoothie; depressed now"). We love to share our lives. We need to share our lives, and social media gives us the chance to do just that.

Here are a few eye-opening statistics about some of the major players in social media:

Facebook is by far the unquestioned king in the social media business, currently boasting almost 850 million registered users (which includes more than half the total population of North America), uploading a total of 250 million photos every day. Additionally, Facebookers click the Like button 2.7 billion times on a daily basis and spend an average of twenty minutes on the site every time they visit. Oh, and if you could get a bird's-eye view of the worldwide web and look at all the page views of the entire Internet all over the world, 20 percent of them would be a Facebook page.

What about Twitter, that other mainstay of oversharing? At the moment, Twitter users send out over 175 million tweets every day, and the microblogging network is growing at a staggering rate, adding roughly one million new accounts on a daily basis. For the record, that's about eleven new accounts created every second.

And then there's YouTube, the place where the occasional gem shines through mountains and mountains of mediocrity. After Google and Facebook, YouTube is the most visited website on the Internet, with a shockingly worldwide reach (only 22 percent of YouTube's traffic is from the United States) and over two billion views per day. YouTube's video count grows by 829,440 videos each day, accounting for about twenty-four hours' worth of video uploaded every minute.[3]

Social networking is growing so exponentially that, between the time I wrote this book and the time my publisher released it, the stats I just gave went out of date.

If our culture's addiction to social media is any indication, we are beyond eager to share what's going on in our lives.

We crave connection.

But instead of sharing in a superficial way online and connecting through bits and bytes and packets of digital information imparted over an Internet connection, where that information can get hijacked or seen by people you don't know, what if we all shared the deepest, darkest parts of our hearts with one or two or three people we trust with absolute certainty?

How safe would you feel then?

Chapter 3

ACCOUNTABILITY IS DEEP

*W*hen you hear the word *Trojan*, what do you think of? If you live in my neck of the woods—that being Pasadena, California—then you probably automatically think of a football team from the University of Southern California that plays a few miles from my house.

And of course, a certain manufacturer of latex-based contraceptives has certainly done a fantastic job aligning the word *Trojan* with their brand. So, there's that.

But a Trojan isn't just a picture of a warrior emblazoned on a condom wrapper or a guy dressed in armor and a funny hat, prancing around on the sidelines at the Los Angeles Coliseum.

One of the most epic battles in the history of storytelling involves Trojans and a certain bit of trickery they fell prey to.

Even if you aren't a major history buff, you have likely heard the story of the Trojan horse and probably know the basics. Big horse. Guys hidden inside it. "Beware of Greeks bearing gifts." Surprise attack. Tide turned. War over.

But the interesting thing about the story of the Trojan horse is not how it ended but how it got to the end, what happened between the time the soldiers hid inside it and the time the city of Troy fell. Because there was a metric ton of people who tried to avoid the outcome they wound up getting.

For starters, you had this guy named Sinon, a Greek warrior who was in on the scheme. He stayed outside the huge wooden horse, pretending to be a disgraced soldier, abandoned by the recently departed Greek army. Sinon's role in the duplicity was to be the guy who would explain the purpose of the faux equestrian idol. His story: the Greeks had built a giant horse as an offering to the goddess Athena, hoping to atone for some serious desecration they'd done to an Athenian temple back in the day. But he upped the ante and threw in this little dig that the Trojans couldn't resist: he said the Greeks made the statue too big for the Trojans to take into their city, meaning that Athena would bless the Greeks instead of the Trojans.

Well, the Trojans couldn't have that! Caught up in their hubris, they pushed, pulled, dragged, and rolled that gigantic wooden horse right on into their city to obtain the blessing of Athena. That'll show those pesky Greeks!

Sinon strolled into the city with them and wound up being interrogated by one of the Trojan priests, a guy named Laocoön. He sniffed out the plot and became the one who uttered that immortal turn of phrase, "Beware of Greeks bearing gifts." Armed with his new knowledge about the deadly trap the Greeks had set for the Trojans, Laocoön set out to warn the Trojan leaders about the cunning plot; but before he could do so, he got an old-fashioned smack down by the Greek god Poseidon, getting him strangled by two sea serpents. These things happen.

But Laocoön was not the only person who got wise to the action. Helen of Troy, she of the beautiful face that launched a thousand ships, also suspected something was up and tried to get the belly-habitating Greeks to tip their hand by standing outside the hollow horse and doing her best impression of their wives. One of the soldiers fell for it and almost gave the game away but was prevented from doing so when Odysseus, the team leader, the Han Solo of this mission to Endor, plugged the soldier's mouth with his fist. The warriors kept their composure and threw Helen off the scent.

One other person figured out ahead of time that the horse was bad news: Cassandra, the king's daughter. She was insistent that the horse would wind up causing the city's downfall, but nobody back then ever listened to a king's daughter, so her warnings went unheeded.

You know the rest: night falls, Greek warriors get out of the horse, they open the gates to the city, the Greek army comes in—*bam, boom, bop* . . . war's over; Greeks win.

The point of this story? If someone wants to get past a wall, they'll figure out a way to get past a wall.

No More Walls

That's why your behavior can't be based solely on walls. Hear me on this because I want to make sure you get exactly what I do mean and not what you think I might mean. It is good to put up safeguards in your life, like in the movie *Raising Arizona*, which features Nicolas Cage as an incorrigible thief with a knack for holding up gas stations, unable to resist his robbing impulses and finding himself bouncing in and out of prison. He does his best to go on the straight and narrow, getting a menial job and working hard, but sometimes, as he puts it, he finds himself "drivin' by convenience stores . . . that weren't on the way home."[1]

We all need to build those barriers, filters, and processes into our daily routines to help us achieve the goals we want to achieve. Want to get out of debt? Lose the credit cards. Want to steer clear of Internet porn? A filter on your web browser is a good start. Want to stay trim? Make sure the fridge is stocked with healthy stuff instead of junk. Want to quit smoking? Find somewhere else to hang out other than your favorite cigarette smoke–filled bar.

So yes, please, by all means make sure you have exterior safeguards in place to help you keep your nose clean on this road we call life.

But I'm just going to tell you, and I speak from experience: if you want to get around a wall, you'll get around that wall.

Credit cards can be cut up, but that doesn't stop the inundation of offers for more of them. Web browser filters are great, but you can almost always find a way around them if you want to. It's a fantastic idea to keep low-calorie foods on hand, but if you really want to cheat on your diet, McDonald's is selling Chicken McNuggets in packs of twenty now. If you're trying to quit smoking, you can avoid the bar . . . and still walk to the corner convenience store.

Just like our friends the Trojans learned at the outset of this chapter, you can have all sorts of voices whispering in your ear that something is a bad idea, trying to warn you away from bad behavior, but that doesn't always keep you from doing it.

And that's where accountability comes in. Because it goes far beyond any rule or barrier, dealing directly with the heart. When you make yourself accountable to one or two or four people, forging a deep, ongoing relationship with them, you begin to alter your internal compass and provide yourself with deeper reasons for living the grand life you want to live instead of the mediocre life that seems inevitable.

Instead of becoming a rule-follower or the type of person who goes right up to the edge of a barrier in order to see what's on the other side of it, the accountable person has an emotional reason to make better choices. Other people—people whom you love and trust—are now fully invested in your life, and when temptation inevitably comes, you can withstand it more gracefully, knowing that your accountability partners will be asking you about it.

And let's get this straight: this has nothing to do with wanting to look good in front of other people. That's just straight-up pride. Instead, accountability has a way of humbling us. We don't point our fingers at ourselves and say, "Check out how awesome I am that I resisted this temptation to do something awful." No, we approach it with humility and gratitude that someone is investing so much time, energy, and love into the innermost parts of our lives. That alone is reason enough to stand strong in the face of tempting choices.

What Accountability Isn't

Before we go any further about what accountability is, I want to make sure we all have an understanding about what accountability is not. There are many, many wrongheaded ideas about what accountability looks like, and many of those ideas stem from an incomplete knowledge of the purpose of accountability and how it works.

So while the rest of this book is about what accountability is, I thought it would be a good idea to take a moment and talk about what it isn't.

For starters, accountability is not "sin management." It isn't about making an inventory of all the bad stuff you've done so that you can guiltily mumble it to your accountability partner and receive your well-deserved shaming and finger-wagging scolding, head hung low in defeat. Sadly, that is the approach quite a few people like to take to accountability, but it is the wrong one. It's not just wrong; it is diametrically opposite of the correct one.

With this "sin management" approach, you put all the emphasis on what you're trying not to do, spinning your entire world into the realm of the negative, placing a restrictive filter over your vision so all you see is the stuff you want to avoid. The problem with that mind-set, though, is that it magnifies the very things you're trying to minimize in your life, making them seem all the more inescapable or even, as we mentioned before, downright inevitable.

Instead of focusing on the problems you want to leave behind you, on the bad habits you want to let go of, accountability helps you focus on the goals you want to achieve. Yes, you need to recognize and avoid obstacles that can trip you up, but if you keep your head down looking for snares and traps, you'll never be able to put your head up and recognize the destination you're headed for.

Because ultimately, that's what accountability is for: to help you achieve some goal that makes your life better. And life always feels better when we're working for something, not against something else. It's better to keep your mind on the benefits of living debt-free than on the difficulties of paying off your credit cards. Yes, you need to pay those off, and you need to have a plan in place to make that happen, but the engine that drives those decisions should be your desire for financial freedom, not a relentless, guilt-inducing, just-don't-spend mentality.

Accountability takes it deeper and puts the focus exactly where it needs to be: on the positive attribute you're trying to attain. And by doing that in a group setting, you have loads of encouragement along the way.

Think of a program like Alcoholics Anonymous. This landmark, history-making organization was started by Bill Wilson and Dr. Robert Smith back in the 1930s when the men simply began to realize that on their own they were powerless against alcohol; but by working together and keeping one another accountable, they could gain the type of strength that comes in numbers, forging a depth that couldn't and wouldn't exist if they tried to go solo. They put the concept to the test, eventually forming twelve principles that would become the basis for Alcoholics Anonymous, as well as other recovery programs all over the world. Millions upon millions of people worldwide have now been helped through the years because these two guys decided to put their focus on the right thing and go deep in their relationships.

My Accountability Continues

Remember the scheduling problem I had, the one I talked about in the previous chapter? I knew that in order to stay on top of all my various speaking engagements and still sow heavily into my family, I had to inject some serious discipline into my calendar. Now, I'm a disciplined guy already, but I knew the temptation to waste time would inevitably arise and that if

I didn't get some help—namely, some accountability—I would succumb to it.

So I reached out. I sent an e-mail to seven different guys, all of them good friends of mine, and opened up to them about all the weight and pressure I was feeling with achieving everything on my calendar that fall. There's a reason I reached out to these particular friends, though: Everyone I contacted happens to be in a similar position as I am—really busy fellows whose work demands pull them in a lot of different directions. I wanted to find out how they did it and whether they felt the same pressure I was feeling every time I opened my calendar on my computer.

Turns out each and every one of them did feel the same way as I did, though none of us was talking to anyone else about it. Well, my feeling is this: the only way anything in this world gets done is if a person or handful of people decide it's worth doing and go through the pains of putting it together, so I decided to take this bull by the horns and help myself and my seven fellow schedule-challenged friends get through this season by encouraging one another.

In other words, we each had a need for some deep accountability in our respective careers, for some encouragement to knuckle down in the midst of difficulty and put our eyes on the goals we wanted to achieve. Our struggles were not identical, but they were similar, and we all recognized how healthy it would be if we could keep one another on track.

Now, when it comes to accountability, someone has to lead it. If you sit around waiting for it to happen, that is pretty much a guaranteed way to make sure nothing happens. You have to step up and make accountability happen in your life, just like I had to step up and make this group happen for me. Yes, the other members of this group weren't necessarily expecting me to call them up and ask them to join an accountability group, so in that sense they were not instigators of this particular means of accountability in their own lives, but they were indeed ready to accept the offer, and all of them were already familiar with accountability—some of them were already in their own groups—before I came knocking on their proverbial doors with my offer.

Here's a quick sidebar: if you're the type of person who feels uncomfortable stepping up to this level of leadership or you just don't have the skill set to do something like that, then I invite you to seek out a program for yourself in your community that helps provide accountability. There's a list of resources at the end of this book that you can consult to help find such things.

Making a Plan

Of course, we all immediately recognized the inherent irony in what we were taking on. It seemed the last thing we really needed to do to straighten out our calendars was to add something else to them. Our schedules were already demanding—why would we include yet another demand on our time and finite resources? Fortunately, these concerns were trumped when we also realized that by holding one another accountable and going deep, we would be making the rest of our time more effective.

I replied to all these e-mails with an idea: What if we met once a week for half an hour? Not in person, but over the phone, through a conference call. (If you're interested in doing this yourself, the service we use is FreeConferenceCall.com, but you can just as easily use Skype, Google Plus, or the AV function in Apple's iChat program; all of these options are free.) What if we built a small bit of time into our packed schedules to encourage one another, check in on one another, and share the things that are tripping us up so we can put our eyes on the true goal?

Everyone agreed they could use just such a thing, and our accountability group was born. We all agreed that accountability wasn't just something we wanted in order to go deep; it was necessary. So let's talk more about that as we head to the next chapter.

Chapter 4

ACCOUNTABILITY IS
NECESSARY

I'm a huge, huge football fan, especially the National Football League. I love it. For the record, I am an unabashed supporter of the Green Bay Packers, and I don't care who knows it. But mostly I just love the game.

We talked earlier about Hurricane Katrina and the way it devastated New Orleans—but one of the great things to come about from that story was the way the city rose up and embraced its football team, the New Orleans Saints, and how that football team embraced the city right back. Less than five years after the hurricane rendered large parts of the city practically unlivable, their hometown team went all the way to the Super Bowl and came back victorious.

No, a Super Bowl title can't rebuild houses and restore lost finances, but it was a nice story to rise out of something so horrendous. It was almost too good to believe.

Unfortunately, though there were many honest achievements on the field that year and some truly jaw-dropping football from many different players, it all has an asterisk next to it thanks to what has come to be widely known as "the bounty scandal."

First, an explanation for the non–sports enthusiasts: a "bounty" is pretty much what it sounds like, except instead of enlisting the services of a long-haired, tanned, sunglasses-wearing fellow who shares a name with a common house pet, defensive coaches offer cash to their players for knocking opposing players out of the game—especially by injury.

After a widespread investigation of the Saints, the National Football League announced that the team's defensive coordinator, Gregg Williams, had indeed instituted a bounty program, handing out cash bonuses in plain envelopes to his players when they surpassed his expectations. Not for performing well and within the rules, but specifically for inflicting harm on opponents.

Over time, the bounty culture became entrenched in the Saints organization, so much so that during the 2009 NFC title game (the winner of which would appear in the Super Bowl), after a vicious hit left Minnesota Vikings quarterback Brett Favre with a sprained ankle, one Saints defensive player jumped up and was caught on a microphone squealing with glee, "Pay me my money!"

Sadly, the news of this scandal has now irreversibly tainted the Saints' improbable Super Bowl win. There were far more players who didn't participate in the bounty system, or who didn't even know about it, than those who did, but now their legacy is irrevocably tied to the actions of a few. That said, whispers of the bounty system—which is against the rules of the NFL—began to make their way up the ladder to the league offices, setting into motion a lengthy investigation.

What really stings about the bounty program is that both the head coach, Sean Payton, and the general manager of the team, Mickey Loomis, apparently knew this was going on and did nothing to put a stop to it. It was this flagrant dismissal of the league rules that led to the Saints receiving the harshest penalty ever handed down to a football team in NFL history: four players responsible for perpetuating bounties were suspended, head coach Sean Payton was suspended for an entire season, and Gregg Williams, the defensive coordinator who started it all, was suspended from the league indefinitely (as of this writing, he has still not been reinstated).

But these penalties could have been avoided entirely if someone had just stepped up and demanded accountability.

Nothing New

The idea of "getting away with" something, an arrogance that permeated every part of the Saints bounty scandal, is nothing new. History is littered with powerful people in powerful positions abusing that power for their own gain . . . and eventual ruin. There is no such thing as a secret that lasts forever—eventually everything comes to light. No dictator in the history of the world, from the very first one all the way to modern-day tyrants like Saddam Hussein or Muammar Gaddafi, has ever managed to keep all their dirty laundry under wraps indefinitely.

The truth always comes out.

What we do counts. It counts to those around us: our spouses, our children, our parents, our friends, and our coworkers.

And the secrets we think we keep? Those will come out, one way or another.

That's why secrets can drive us crazy, causing us to constantly look over our shoulders and worry about being found out. Or, alternately, we can become overconfident when we don't get found out, and then we take our secret lives up to the next level, working extra hard at ruining the things and people around us we love the most.

This is the great thing about getting accountable: when we make ourselves accountable to others, we have a place to air those secrets so they can't control us. Can't ruin us. Can't bring us down.

Accountability is a necessary part of living, all in the name of prevention.

The Password Problem

My kids are currently ten years old and seven years old, and since we are a family that embraces technology, they currently have iPods, which they mostly use for listening to music (my son especially is really into Justin Bieber) and for playing the occasional game.

If you don't know anything about the way iPods work (or iPhones and iPads, for that matter), I'll need to catch you up to speed on an important part of this story: when you get one of these devices, you create a password-protected account with Apple to be able to buy and download applications from their App Store. This where you get all those games and other tools to use on your iPod.

Any time you buy something from the App Store, you have to enter the password to your account as an extra layer of safety to prevent you from accidentally buying things with a way-ward swipe of your finger or to prevent your children from buying things with intentional swipes of their fingers.

When I got the iPods for my kids, I set them up with a single account and a password that only I knew so I could manage their iPods for them and make sure they didn't buy some ninety-nine-dollar app where you feed fish and hope they don't die.

Well, guess what? My son figured out the password.

He immediately started freaking out, just thinking about and contemplating the enormous power he could now wield over his iPod. No longer any need to wait for Dad to punch in the password to update his apps. No need to run any future purchases through the funnel of the father; instead, he and his sister could live it up on their own.

It wasn't long before my daughter told me that my son had figured out the password, so my wife and I had to figure out what to do about it. My wife suggested that I change the password, but after putting some thought into it, I decided to let it stay, and here's why.

My kids know where I keep the keys to my car, but I don't ever worry that they're going to nab them and go for a joyride. My kids know where to find my wallet, but I don't live in fear that they will go on an Amazon spending spree with my debit or credit cards.

I don't have those fears because, in both those cases, there would be a tangible evidence that is impossible to ignore. My car would have less gas and more miles on it (and presumably more dents in the fenders), or we would have UPS knocking on our door delivering boxes of DVDs or every Batman LEGO set. My kids are smarter than that.

Plus, they know it's wrong.

So I decided to bring in my son and daughter and tell them I wasn't changing the password to their accounts on their iPods. "But," I said, "you know the rules: you aren't allowed to buy anything on your own without my approval first. And if you buy something, know that I'll get an e-mail from the App Store telling me what you bought and how much it cost, and the day I get that e-mail is the last day you have an iPod."

So far, it's working.

Eventually, my kids will be old enough to have their own accounts, with their own passwords linked to their own money, and they'll have the opportunity to buy whatever they want. My hope is that I can demonstrate to them now how freeing it is to live a life with no secrets, with no fear of being found out.

A Reputation Ruined on a Red-Eye

Here's another story: as I was in the midst of writing this book, a minor dustup took place on the Internet when an actor named Brian struck up a conversation with a sharp-witted model named Melissa while they sat next to each other on a red-eye flight between New York and Los Angeles.

Now, ordinarily this seems to be a premise straight out of a romantic comedy: handsome actor and winsome model hit it off at thirty-five thousand feet, and love and laughter ensue, right?

Well, maybe the laughter. Though not for everyone. And certainly not for Brian.

Because there's a wrinkle in this story that seems all the more fitting in our social media–drenched era. See, according to Melissa, Brian's conversation was laced with all sorts of stereotypical actor-speak (he called their conversation a "collabo" and referred to their collective pairing as "artists like us") that it almost turned into a parody of the jargon. Melissa found this to be humorous and started quoting Brian on her Twitter account, describing their conversation and peppering it with her own barb-filled asides.

Now, we only know Melissa's side of the story, through her tweets, but what went down next doesn't make Brian look good. According to Melissa's Twitter feed, Brian's awkward banter tipped into the realm of flirtation (assisted, presumably, from the beer he was consuming onboard the plane), which would have been fine except that Brian had been married for almost ten years at the time and had recently given an interview to *Christianity Today* about how he had reached his rock-bottom after battling alcohol and steroids and had found strength to clean up through faith in God.

Uh-oh.

Soon afterward, the story went viral, and Brian issued the standard "Wow, this is such a crazy, made-up story; let's put it behind us and never talk about it again!" message through his Facebook fan page, and more mainstream organizations started to pick up the story.

But one thing that Melissa tweeted really boils down the essence of it all:

"Did I just ruin [Brian's] life via Twitter?"

Personally, I believe that Brian, in a moment of weakness, succumbed to his addiction, thinking no one would ever know. I believe he thought he could have a secret beer or two, secretly turn on the charm with the pretty young brunette sitting next to him, and then see what happened next. I don't think he necessarily was hoping to have a full-on fling with her; I think he was looking for a little validation. As a man, though I can't endorse those kinds of actions, I can understand the motivation behind them.

But he thought no one would ever know.

He thought it would stay a secret.

He thought the truth wouldn't come out.

But it does. It always does. Sometimes it comes out sooner rather than later, but you can count on your secrets not remaining secrets forever. So instead of keeping secrets, get accountable.

Cover-ups and Catastrophes

One of the lies we tell ourselves when we decide to go off-track is that age-old canard, "No one has to know," or its close cousin, "No one will ever find out." But then things inevitably spiral out of control, and the secrets come to the surface.

When talking about the unearthing of a secret life, I automatically think of Tiger Woods, who rose in ranking through the early 2000s until he was on top of the world as the greatest professional golfer of this age or possibly any other, but who is also a very secretive, walled-off type of person. He's a nightmare for journalists to cover because he is neither enthusiastic nor profuse in the information he offers up to their questions (which he generally seems to consider inane and bothersome).

Here's a fascinating (and kind of petty) story about Tiger Woods that was revealed in the book *The Big Miss* by Woods's former caddy Hank Haney.[1] As often happens between golfers and caddies, the two became semi-friends and spent a lot of time together, mostly working on Woods's game but sometimes just hanging out. Haney details a story in his book where the two would eat dinner together at Woods's house and then sit down to watch television (usually *SportsCenter*).

Woods had an eccentric love of sugar-free Popsicles, and he would generally hop up during a commercial break to grab himself a Popsicle out of the freezer. No big deal, right? But Haney soon discovered that no matter how many times this happened, Woods would never offer Haney a Popsicle.

Now, obviously, this is not earth-shattering news, and the

revelation of Woods's selfish hoarding of Popsicles is nothing along the lines of the bombshell that exploded later in his life. The story is interesting, though, as a snapshot of Woods's mentality and his inward-focused view of himself. The man was so intense that even Haney, his caddy and confidant, felt awkward and distressed at the thought of asking to have a Popsicle. He eventually did, and Woods told him he could grab one if he wanted it; but even after that, Woods never offered Haney a Popsicle. That's how closed off his world was.

But that insular world came crashing down in late 2009 when allegations began to pop up of marital infidelity. First it was a nightclub manager in New York City. Then a waitress. Then other women began to pipe up saying they'd had affairs with Woods, and by then, the deluge was too large to contain. It became a classic example of the old journalistic saying, "Where there's smoke, there's fire."

Woods finally came clean and admitted his transgressions in early 2010, but by then the damage had been done—his sponsors began dropping him left and right, and he lost many lucrative endorsement deals with Gatorade, General Motors, AT&T, Accenture, Gillette, and watchmaker TAG Heuer—to an estimated tune of somewhere between $5 billion and $12 billion. Even worse, he also lost his marriage when his wife, Elin, divorced him that August.

For a tight-lipped guy, Tiger Woods's admission was surprisingly candid and honest, as well as a fascinating glimpse into the minds of those with secret lives: "I thought I could get away with whatever I wanted to. I felt that I had worked hard my entire life and deserved to enjoy all the temptations around me. I felt I was entitled. Thanks to money and fame, I didn't have to go far to find them. I was wrong. I was foolish."[2]

Tiger Woods was allowed to have a secret life because of the power that comes with being one of the wealthiest, most well-known athletes in the world. But even all that money and fame were not enough to keep his secrets. He is still playing golf and is even returning to his winning form, but there will always be asterisks next to his name now, thanks to his indiscretions and his secret life.

Or what about Arnold Schwarzenegger? This is another man who was on top of the world—an international film star who parlayed his immense popularity into enough political swagger to get elected governor of California. But all that time he was sitting on a secret: He had carried on an affair with a woman who worked in his house, and he had fathered a child with her, a child born in 1997, just a week or so after the birth of Schwarzenegger's son with his wife, Maria Shriver.

Arnold attempted to cover up his responsibility by quietly seeing that his love child and the mother were cared for financially, all while keeping that secret son in the dark about his father's role in bringing the child into the world. Arnold would pop into the boy's life occasionally, attending his baptism or teaching him how to play golf, but the lad had no idea who his father was until the spring of 2011, when the *Los Angeles Times* published a bombshell story about Schwarzenegger's indiscretion. By then, the boy was almost fifteen years old.

The exposure of the story took its toll on the family, and Schwarzenegger and Shriver destroyed their twenty-five-year marriage.

Arnold had managed to cover up his role in fathering a love child for fifteen years, but that wasn't long enough.

The truth will come out.

One more example, and one that is truly tragic in terms of lives affected. You may remember a dashing senator from the state of North Carolina named John Edwards, who came out of nowhere in the early 2000s to become a rising star in politics. He campaigned for the office of the president of the United States in 2004, eventually losing the nomination to John Kerry, but then was promptly chosen as Kerry's running mate. The pair lost the election that year to George W. Bush and Dick Cheney, but Edwards continued his political career undaunted, trying once more for the presidency in 2008.

Everything seemed to be going well for this handsome, well-spoken politician. Then came the news that his wife, Elizabeth, had been diagnosed once more with breast cancer, an illness she had been treated for and defeated previously. The cancer came back, though, and in a big way.

In the midst of all this, more news came out about the way John Edwards had been living his life: he had been having an extramarital affair with a campaign worker named Rielle Hunter. At first Edwards denied the allegations, but the mere fact of their existence damaged his reputation in political circles, not to mention his ability to get elected by popular vote. The other guy would have to be pretty dismal for people to vote instead for the candidate who cheated on his wife while she had cancer.

But, like Arnold Schwarzenegger, things got worse for Edwards when it was discovered that Rielle Hunter had given birth to a child in 2008, a daughter she claimed Edwards had fathered. Around this time, Edwards admitted to the affair but denied being the father of this little girl. There were some salvos fired back and forth between the Edwards and Hunter camps about paternity suits and DNA tests and whatnot, but before it came to that, Edwards finally admitted that, yes, he was indeed the father of Rielle Hunter's child.

So far, all these sordid details are covering the same ground as the Tiger Woods and Arnold Schwarzenegger stories, but now John Edwards's story takes a turn for the worse. Because in 2009, the United States Department of Justice began an investigation that lasted a total of two years and that culminated in a grand jury indictment for Edwards, alleging that he had used more than a million dollars in campaign funds to cover up his affair with Hunter.

His official charges were all felonies and included charges for collecting illegal campaign contributions, conspiracy, and making false statements. Edwards was facing as many as thirty years in prison if convicted and, on top of that, a fine of up to $1.5 million.

John Edwards was found not guilty on one of the charges against him, and the other five were declared as mistrials; those charges were subsequently dropped, and Edwards is now a free man.

But how free is he really?

How free are any of these three men?

Imagine what Tiger Woods and Arnold Schwarzenegger and John Edwards were living with. Imagine the type of psychological weight they carried with them every day, the knowledge of what was going on in secret, what they were doing or had done behind closed doors (or the weight they're *still* carrying as they deal daily with the fallout from their actions). Every time Tiger traveled, every time Arnold saw a photo of his illegitimate son, every time John Edwards made another stump speech, they likely felt a crushing remorse that demanded a response (unless they're emotionless sociopaths incapable of discerning right from wrong, which is unlikely). And that response would've been an even more crushing compartmentalization in their souls to allow them to continue living.

Imagine how scared they must've been almost every moment of the day, worried about the eventual reckoning they would experience, the day the news would break and the world would know the truth.

Or perhaps they were living in a constant state of adrenaline, getting a rush or kick out of getting away with whatever they thought they were getting away with. Maybe these guys fed their egos off the notion that the walls around them were impenetrable and that their power could be wielded effortlessly and absolutely.

What does that do to a person? What kind of life is that to live?

The Difference Accountability Makes

In all three of these examples, we have men who were able to transpose their power, money, and fame onto elaborate secret-keeping operations that only temporarily staved off the inevitable. My question is, where were the people who were supposed to be keeping Tiger Woods and Arnold Schwarzenegger and John Edwards accountable? Did any of these men have people in their lives in whom they could confide? Did they have a support system to help them stay on track personally, or were they just surrounded by yes-men and hangers-on?

How different would their lives be if they'd had someone like that?

What relationships would've been restored? Would they still have their marriages today? Would they still have their reputations? Would Tiger Woods still be the transcendent, dominant golfer he used to be? Would Arnold Schwarzenegger have an influence on this world other than lending a little box office appeal to the *Expendables* movies or cashing in once more on the *Terminator* franchise? Would John Edwards be president?

In general, the more well-known you are, the more you tend to remove people from your sphere of influence who don't agree with you, the people who call you out on your stupid stuff.

A Friend to the Famous

I mentioned earlier that my son is a huge fan of Justin Bieber, and as a result, I have inhaled a lot of secondhand information about this talented musical phenomenon. I appreciate the way this Bieber kid goes about his business, especially when it comes to keeping himself grounded. Even though he has a manager (who at one point provided Bieber with a "swagger coach"), he has a good friend named Ryan who goes on the road with him. Not a celebrity, not a person schooled in the ways of popularity or the press.

Just a friend from high school.

This isn't a kid who wants something; this kid is not a hanger-on or the member of some money-grubbing posse; he's just a kid who was friends with Justin Bieber before he became famous and who remains friends with him.

In a way, he keeps Bieber accountable, keeps him grounded and real—so that even when Bieber gets pulled over on a Los Angeles freeway for speeding in an electric sports car that costs more than a hundred grand, in order to evade a swarm of paparazzi, he can quickly come back down to earth and get back to living his life.

Let the stories of these four men serve as a small example to you: accountability would've changed so, so much in their lives. That's why it's a necessity.

My Group Gets Formal

Back to the story of my own accountability group. We knew that in order for it to work in a half-hour window once a week, we couldn't waste time with small talk or catching up on

families or discussing the previous night's basketball game—
we had to get down to business, and quickly.

In order to help facilitate that promptness, I created a
questionnaire that I posted in a special spot online that only
members of our group could access. This list of questions
was simple and easy to fill out, but it contained the questions
we wanted to be asked—the idea being that the night before,
you filled out your answers and sent them to everyone else in
the group. That way, each person got a chance to see how you
answered and could hold your feet to the fire during the call
the next day.

But it didn't stop there: it wouldn't make sense for me to try
to write questions that applied across the board to everyone. I
knew I had things in my life I needed to be held accountable
for that other guys in the group wouldn't, like going on a date
night with my wife once a week or taking time three or four
days a week to work out. Some of those other guys were workout fiends—they didn't need to be asked about it.

One more piece of business: to help add an extra dose of
accountability to the phone call itself, we made a rule that
the last person to dial into the conference call (the number of
which I'd set up through a free conference-call service) had
to run the meeting the following week. That gave everyone
an incentive to try to be punctual when it came to dialing the
phone, helping us all be on time so we didn't waste even a few
minutes of our call.

The beauty of filling out the questionnaires ahead of time
was that everyone came to the meeting prepared, so as soon

as we all chimed in on the call and let everyone know were all there, the moderator could look at my report from the night before and say, "Okay, Craig, I see that you only worked out once this week instead of three times, and you also didn't have a date night with your wife. What's up with that? What's going on?" And that gave me an opportunity to talk about what indeed was going on, that I had let my schedule get away from me and had overlooked a night my wife and I could've gone on a date, or how I'd just gotten lazy (because I really hate working out) and had decided to sleep in one morning instead of getting up and hitting the gym.

And I did all that stuff knowing I would be asked about it. And that I would continue to be asked about it. So, knowing full well that these guys were going to keep pestering me about my exercise habits, it made it harder to ignore the alarm and sleep through my usual workout time or not to plan at least a couple of hours one evening to spend time with just my wife.

Of course, if I wanted to, I could lie on my questionnaire the night before and be all, "Nothing to see here! Everything's great!" But that would defeat the entire purpose of accountability. Again, I wasn't trying to avoid getting into trouble—I was trying to achieve the goal of managing my schedule with aplomb. And even beyond that, it wasn't really about that—I mean, that was a side benefit to what I was hoping to accomplish; I just needed help. We all needed help. We needed one another because all of us in this group are the type of guys who tend to take on too much and wind up needing one another's input and wisdom in order to make it through the day, through the week, through the month. I needed help and wisdom and encouragement from these guys, and to get that, I needed to be honest about the obstacles I was facing.

Plus, it's easier to be honest about those types of things when you have a group of people who have agreed to sit next to you in a support role, not across from you like an angry police chief threatening to revoke your badge.

One of the interesting things I've noticed as I've walked through this accountability group (as well as the group I had in my adolescence with my youth pastor and my friend Jake) was the type of questions I needed to be asked. When I was meeting with Tom before school at McDonald's, I had no need to answer any questions about having a date night with my wife. That was nothing that was even remotely in the picture yet. But I did need to be asked (if I'm being completely honest) whether I'd masturbated that week, and that's a question that remains on the list to this day and probably will for the rest of my life.

I guess the point is that there are going to be some questions that come and go from your list, and others that stay on there your whole life. If you're trying to lose weight or get out of debt, then you have an achievable, measurable goal with a definite end point—it may take you years to get to your target weight or to get to a point where you're debt-free, but you will get there eventually. And once you do, you probably don't need to be asked each week whether you stopped at the fast-food place on your way to work to get a sausage biscuit or used your credit card for a spontaneous purchase. You may have to get asked those questions every now and then to make sure you stay on top of something that used to hold you down, but they'll eventually fall off the list.

But if you're wanting to, say, continue learning something new, to always be expanding your horizons and your level of knowledge and experience about the world, then that's a question you could probably stand to get asked every time: What did you learn this week that you didn't already know? That would be an incentive to dig into that library book on your nightstand before bed instead of watching more *Seinfeld* reruns that you've seen already and can quote better than Jerry Seinfeld himself.

With that in mind, I've changed my questions over the years, and as many of them drop off the list, just as many pop on. There are always areas of my life where I need work, but, once again, that's a good thing. The questions I want to be asked flow from a positive mind-set. I don't approach accountability from a mind-set that says, "Keep me from doing something bad." I've learned to turn that around and make it come from a mind-set that says, "Help me do something good."

That's why accountability is so very necessary, for each of our lives. Especially in today's culture where we're constantly being told about the smallest foibles of those around us. There are cameras everywhere, capturing everything, and it isn't hard to look at this world negatively, just waiting for people to trip up.

When we get accountable, we lessen that point of view in our own minds, and tripping up seems less inevitable. We walk with our heads held high, knowing that we can stroll freely and unashamed because we have accountability right beside us, helping us, supporting us, keeping us honest and secure.

But what does accountability take? What do we need to put into it in order to get something out of it? Let's find out as we continue our journey together toward accountability.

Part 2

WHAT

What does accountability require?
Everything . . .

Chapter 5

YOU NEED HONESTY

*N*ow we have come to the scary part: putting accountability into action. It's going to take some work on your behalf, and that work has to start with some serious honesty. I'm not talking about telling yourself that everything's okay when it's not; I'm talking about taking a step back, getting an overview of your life, and really examining it with the cold detachment of a world-weary, seen-it-all TV coroner.

Except you don't have to be the only one to make that assessment. You also get the honor of presenting your life—every glimmering achievement and every stinking secret part of it—to a couple of people you love and trust. Your accountability partners.

And that's where the honesty really comes in.

But as the saying goes, you can't be half-pregnant, and you can't expect accountability to work if you don't go all the way down the street to complete and total honesty.

If that sounds tough, there's a reason for that: it *is* tough. But here's the good news: your accountability partners are doing the exact same thing. They're examining the difficult parts of their lives and sharing them with you. You get to work together to keep each other honest and accountable. And with that comes a wonderful amount of freedom that you could never imagine on your own.

Can I tell you a story? This is a story that takes place in London, England, a few hundred years ago, which is mind-boggling to some of us Americans, since our country wasn't even a country yet at the time of this story. Anyway, this was long before digital scales or even those round, hanging scales you see at the supermarket in the produce section, with the big red needle that helpfully tells you exactly how many pounds of kiwis you have. Back at the time of our story, scales were balance-style, like the kind you see Lady Justice holding out from her blindfolded face in statues in front of courthouses around the world.

Those types of scales operated based on a set of weights—you'd put the "one pound" weight on one side then load up the other side with cabbages or mutton or what-have-you until the scales balanced. Voila: one pound of mutton.

Except it wasn't always exactly a pound because those types of scales were extraordinarily easy to manipulate. Take a weight labeled "one pound," shave a couple of ounces off the bottom, and now you're handing out fourteen ounces of mutton at the one-pound price. More profits for you, and you only have to gyp your customers and be a little dishonest.

In the midst of this parade of cheating and wheeling and dealing, a couple of London grocers got together and decided to be honest with each other. They agreed that it was best for their customers and for their reputations if they had honest scales—aside from the fact that it was the right thing to do—so they hatched a plan. They would regularly check each other's scales. Once a week, one grocer went to the other and made sure all his weights balanced out, and then the first grocer got his weights assessed by the second one.

Guess what happened? Customers found out what was going on, word began to spread around town that you could trust these two grocers to have honest scales, and their businesses began to thrive. And you know how business works—if something is paying off for one guy, all the other guys in the same business start trying it out. (Just look at how many iPhone copies are out there now, even though touch-screen technology existed long before the iPhone made it popular.) Other London grocers decided to join in the fun and began having their scales assessed, and all these grocers eventually banded together to form a sort of loose trade association that was called—I'm not making this up here—the Most Worshipful Company of Livery Merchants.

Well, soon enough, other non-grocer merchants began hearing about this swell idea and decided to use it among themselves, and then the people in charge of the government got wind of it and thought it sounded like a good deal, and if you work in the modern-day UK National Measurement Office, then you have a couple of medieval grocers to thank for your job.

See what a little honesty can do?

Honesty in Action

One of my favorite journalists these days is Anderson Cooper (and while we're on the subject, Martin Bashir is no slouch either). I had the privilege and honor of appearing on his show on CNN once and have always felt Cooper is a guy who is dedicated to being fair to everyone who comes on his show and making sure that all relevant sides of the story are heard so that his viewers can draw accurate conclusions about the story and how it affects them personally.

One of my favorite segments that Cooper regularly has on his show is called "Keeping Them Honest," which is generally a short look at a claim made by some politician or other newsworthy party, and then following that up with factual information to see whether they were being honest or not. It's a fascinating segment to watch, especially when he brings in a guest in person. He'll typically show a clip of the person saying something outlandish, then present him or her with facts showing that perhaps the claim was a bit off the mark, and then give the person a chance to explain exactly what he or she meant.

Not only is it entertaining television to watch these people squirm under the lights of truth and honesty, but it's compelling to see those lights being shined at all. Honesty seems to be something that many in our society are all too happy to live without, preferring instead rigorous ideology that lines up with their own personal worldview or that allows them to skate around truths they find inconvenient.

But, of course, honesty is not necessarily a virtue in the political realm—plausibility, believability, and a good applause line or sound bite are the currencies there. That's why I appreciate the work of Anderson Cooper or Martin Bashir, or even Jon Stewart and Stephen Colbert, journalists (or, in the case of Stewart and Colbert, entertainers posing as journalists, but with more journalistic integrity than some actual journalists and talking heads have) who insist on pointing out the foibles and inconsistencies of the narratives we hear from those in authority and power, or even of the narratives we tell ourselves.

In short, these people are doing exactly what Cooper advertises: keeping us all honest.

Not Yes-Men

While honesty with yourself is an important trait to possess, it's critical not just to be honest in your own outlook but also to surround yourself with people who are unafraid to be honest with you. It feels great to bring people into your life who will rubber-stamp every thought you have, who will tell you yes anytime you ask for something or have an idea. But those are not the kinds of people who will help you move forward—indeed, they'll only hold you back.

We need people in our lives who will disagree with us, challenge us, and cause us to really consider where we're coming from, where we are, and where we're going. As our ministry, called Fireproof Ministries (XXXchurch.com is technically an offshoot of Fireproof), has grown and developed, we've had to put together a board of directors in order to help govern it and to achieve and maintain our status as a not-for-profit entity. I had a couple of directions I could have gone when asking people to serve on that board of directors: I could have stocked it with yes-men and asked friends who would enthusiastically embrace anything I come up with, or I could have sought out the service of people who would approach their position with thoughtfulness and stewardship.

I went with the latter. I wanted people on the Fireproof Ministries' board of directors who would be comfortable telling me no when the situation demanded it. I already have enough people in my life telling me yes—I didn't need the same thing when I went to the board.

My problem is that I have a new idea practically every morning when I roll out of bed. I'm always thinking of new ways to spread the message of what we do, of outside-the-box ways to reach people who would not normally be reached with the message of XXXchurch, of shaking up the establishment and provoking a little thought here and there. That's one of my gifts, and it's one that has served me well.

But I also have to put people in my life who will help me

accept my own limitations, whether they be time or money or scheduling or relationships or whatever. I need to have a board of directors that will stand up to my relentless hatching of ideas in a friendly but direct way. I need people whom I have a good relationship with, who are even friends of mine, whom I can put in a position of trust and authority, and who will say, "Craig, that idea is terrible." Or even better: "You know what, Craig, that's a good idea, but we don't have the money for it. And besides, you need to concentrate on finishing the idea you had yesterday."

I need honest people.

I don't need people who are afraid of hurting my feelings or who will be worried about sending me into a depressed spiral if they tell me no. I need people who will do the right thing—the honest thing—because it is the right and honest thing to do.

In fact, when I was writing the leadership documentation for Fireproof Ministries, specifically the part that defines the powers of the board of directors, I set myself up as the executive director of the organization and then gave the board of directors the power to vote me out if they saw fit. Now, that sounds scary, but if they don't have the power to fire me, then who does? And if they can't fire me, then what's the point of having a board of directors in the first place?

If there are no consequences, then there's no accountability.

The board of directors can't fire me on a whim—it wouldn't be an easy process (it would require a unanimous vote)—but it is a plausible possibility, and that knowledge helps to keep me honest in all my dealings. I didn't want to set up my own little kingdom, like so many churches and corporations do now, stocking the boards of directors with other pastors and CEOs who will in turn put me on their boards of directors, allowing for one small-minded circle of people who can pat one another on the back and vote for massive pay raises for everyone in their circle.

No, I wanted a board of directors with some teeth, with people who were unafraid to tell me no and who, if I got really crazy with my behavior to the point where it started to damage the ministry, could put me out on the street and install someone else who would do some good.

It keeps me honest.

Before we go on, let's make sure you understand exactly where I'm coming from: I am not some masochist who assembled a board of directors who will beat me down or give me a tongue-lashing every time I approach them with a new idea. I am not saying that "honesty" is the same thing as "policing," especially because there are way, way too many people out there looking for reasons to tear others down, or who see accountability as a way to step up onto a high horse and feel better about themselves by making their accountability partners feel worse.

That's not honesty—that's legalism.

Say No to Yes-Men

While we're on the subject of yes-men, I want to share a take on them written by my friend Ryan Russell. Ryan works for

XXXchurch and Fireproof Ministries and has a great knack for pulling leadership qualities out of people.

Just don't talk to Ryan about yes-men. It doesn't get pretty. His words:

There is a significant difference between leading underneath someone else and being a "yes man." Leading underneath (second chair, vice-presidency, COO, employee down the chain) affords you every bit of latitude to have conviction, strength, expertise, great people skills, critical decision making opportunities, and more.

Being a "yes man," only doing what you think you ought to in order to keep your job through kissing up to your boss, will inevitably end with several outcomes:

1. Your direct reports will not see you for a leader but merely as a middle man, a spineless manager. You will garner no respect.
2. You will never experience the results that your boss really expects and hopes for.
3. You will ultimately be deemed unnecessary and be fired.
4. No one who has employed you or worked for you will give you a solid reference for your next gig.

So however much you think you will get ahead by being a yes-man, you might as well go ahead and risk being a real leader because the rewards are greater. However, the journey of leadership is a lot more fun and self-respecting!

So that's Ryan's take on being a yes-man (which, by the way, I borrowed with his permission from his blog, RedBikeLeader .com[1]).

I cannot say this or stress this enough: every facet of accountability must be seasoned with grace and love. You can't look at your accountability partner and say, "That habit is disgusting—what's wrong with you?" Then you are just being mean-spirited and are actually doing the opposite of what you're trying to accomplish. Calling people out on stuff can be done with discretion, tact, and love—it doesn't have to be blunt and harsh, a slap in the face veiled in some sort of "I'm just being honest" piety. There's no room for that mentality within the framework of accountability. Or life, really.

No, when you open yourself to honesty—whether you're on the giving end or the receiving end—you are granting permission to someone else to ask or answer the tough questions, and you have to be willing to go along with them as far as they do—to answer or ask those same tough questions of them and of yourself.

That's the only way honesty will work within accountability.

Can't Fake It

The long and short of accountability is this: it only works if you're honest. You can't fake your way through accountability because, if you do, then what's the point? Who are you trying to kid? If your accountability partners ask you a question, and you don't answer honestly, you're . . . what? Trying to look good to the one or two or four people who will love and accept you just as you are, flaws and all? And now you're going to lie to them?

If you can't be honest with your accountability partner, then who can you be honest with?

And if you aren't being honest with them, are you being honest with yourself?

Sadly, there are a lot of people who fake it. Who fake life, who fake their personality, who fake their recovery, and who fake their way through accountability.

When I was a kid, the summer of 1990 was my ultimate summer. I absolutely love going to concerts—there's something about the energy and vitality of a live show that I can't get enough of—and that love of concertgoing was born that fateful summer of 1990. That year I saw Young MC (remember his big singles "Bust a Move" and "Principal's Office"? That was a younger, gentler time for hip-hop), Debbie Gibson (her big hits were "Foolish Beat," "Out of the Blue," "Shake Your Love," "Only in My Dreams," and "Lost in Your Eyes," and yeah, of course I had a crush on her), and, the cream of the crop, the very first concert I ever saw, Milli Vanilli.

Now, in case you happen to have been under a pop culture rock, Milli Vanilli rocketed to instant stardom on the backs of their singles "Girl You Know It's True," "Baby Don't Forget My Number," and the ultimate in radio ballads, "Blame It on the Rain." Of course, their model-ready looks, uniquely braided long hair, and superfly dance moves in the relatively new medium of the music video didn't hurt their appeal.

The duo won a Grammy for Best New Artist, as well as a lot of acclaim from fans. They were on top of the world.

Until it was revealed that they'd been faking it.

A producer had put together the group using vocals from talented singers who, while they had good pipes, were, in his estimation, not very marketable from an image standpoint. He wanted front men who were easier on the eyes, so he hired a pair of French models named Rob Pilatus and Fabrice Morvan to lip-synch the songs in the videos and onstage.

The music-buying public felt like they'd been swindled, and the Grammy was revoked. The duo, once on the path to stardom, was now in shambles and was quickly dumped into the wastebasket of has-beens and trivia answers. The story of Milli Vanilli took a more tragic turn almost a decade later when, as the front men, Rob and Fab, were exploring the possibilities of putting together a comeback tour, one of them (Pilatus) was found dead of an apparent drug overdose in a German hotel.

The Internal Strength of Honesty

I've known people who lie to themselves, who try to fake out their own conscience, and who have been successful, at least for a time. I've known more than one person who has been struggling with using online pornography and who sought out accountability to help them stay clean—usually by setting up x3Watch on their computer and then engaging the help of a friend or trusted relative to list as their accountability partner—only to then convince themselves, *Well, I'm all set up to be accountable for Internet porn so . . . off to the strip club!*

That is not a joke. I'm serious. I've met people who actually think that way. And not just the Las Vegas friends I mentioned in the introduction to this book. I have other friends who are compartmentalizing their accountability to perverse degrees. Friends who are just trying—and successfully, I might add—to fool themselves.

But if you're going to grow as a person—if you're going to become an organized person or someone who puts aside distractions to spend more time with the ones you love, if you're going to have a better diet or put aside addictive behaviors, or whatever you want to do to grow—then you have to be honest. The raw kind of honesty that digs deep and opens up those scary closet doors in our minds to clean out whatever cobwebs or spooky monsters we might find there.

Accountability requires the internal strength of honesty. We have to be strong enough to hear the honest questions and answer them honestly. We have to be strong enough to ask honest questions and hear honest answers, reacting appropriately and with grace and respect.

Without honesty, there is no accountability, pure and simple.

Hearing Honest Answers

What if you're the one asking the tough questions, and your accountability partner confides in you with even tougher honesty? What if they tell you that they're having an affair with a coworker? Maybe they aren't having sex with them or haven't even been remotely intimate with them, but they are confiding in them and have started running to this coworker with their emotional problems and crying on their understanding shoulder. What do you do?

What if your accountability partner tells you that their obsession with getting slim has gone too far and now they've developed an eating disorder? What do you do?

What if they do what someone did to another friend of mine, avoiding the accountability meeting for weeks and then finally blindsiding you with an explanation why: because they've been attending meetings for Gamblers Anonymous? What do you do?

What if they are one of the people I mentioned earlier who joyously proclaim that they haven't looked at porn all week but have dropped a hundred bucks on lap dances at the strip club? What do you do?

There are two major questions you must consider before we go any further. The first is this: Are you ready to hear honest answers?

And the follow-up question to that is this one: What do you do then?

How do you confront someone in love? How do you hold their feet to the fire and encourage them to change while still demonstrating that you are on their side?

How do you keep them honest while staying honest with yourself?

It's extremely easy for an accountability relationship to turn into a sort of gossip fest, where you listen eagerly, mouth dripping with saliva, hanging on every salacious detail—but that's not what accountability calls for. It calls for a measured, direct, honest, grace-filled response. You have to be a safe place for honest confession, and that means you must receive any jaw-dropping revelations appropriately, with your jaw squarely undropped.

Don't fly off the handle in condemnation and derision. I can't say this enough: you aren't there to sit across from them in judgment; you're there to sit next to them in support. Whatever honest thing they've shared with you, whether it's a revelation that they're gay or as mundane as an admission that they left dishes in the sink overnight, it's a part of their lives they have entrusted with you. You owe it to them to take care of that part and to show them through your words, your facial expressions, your body language, and your subsequent actions that they can trust you with every part of their story, including the shocking parts.

Does that mean you don't act on it? Of course not. If they've done something illegal or something horrendously transgressive, you have to take some kind of action. If they're cheating on their spouse or doing damage to their children, that requires a response, and I can't tell you exactly what that response would or should be—you'd have to feel that out for yourself.

I will say this: if you are in a relationship with someone and are also friends with their spouse, and they have something going on that's hindering their marriage, then sometimes you're going to have to draw the line and throw out an ultimatum. Something like, "I'm going to keep asking you about this and whether you've talked about it with your spouse, and if you refuse to bring it up with them, then believe me—I will." I've had to do that before, and though it was extremely uncomfortable, it was worth it.

Look, I'm just talking about the ways we should act when we're in an accountability relationship. We have to think about what honesty looks like from both sides of this equation, and make sure we're prepared to enact it. No matter what.

Honesty in My Group

When I put together my schedule-oriented group of guys to meet on a conference call, one of the big leaps of faith I took was to include people I knew, who all had a direct connection to me personally, but who did not necessarily know one another. I wondered initially whether that lack of personal knowledge would create inhibitions in some of the guys— I mean, how comfortable would you feel talking about your struggles with someone you don't even know, but who a friend of yours assures you is okay and safe?

It became clear early on that for this to work as well as we needed it to, we had to get to know one another a lot better. There was no way we would feel free to be completely honest without that foundational knowledge of one another's stories.

So one of the things we initiated was an underlying policy

of connection—that each of us had to connect with at least one other person in the group once a week, outside of our regular half-hour phone call. It didn't have to be the same person each week; in fact, we encouraged one another to connect with different people in the group, just to help get to know everyone. In a group of seven guys, there's plenty of storytelling and potential connection to go around.

But we also decided early into the life of this group that we needed to dig deeply into one another's stories, and the only way to do that was to meet up in person. I don't remember who had the idea initially, but once it was suggested, we all loved it. Though we all lived in different cities, we decided to take a weekend to meet up in the same town and just hang out. It would give each member of the group the opportunity to tell his story in-depth, and it would go a long way to helping us feel safe enough with one another to be as honest as we needed to be.

So it was on. We looked at our already-packed schedules, found a weekend that worked for all of us, and booked it. I was living in Las Vegas at the time, so we agreed to meet there. Yeah, I know what that sounds like—seven red-blooded guys getting together for a weekend in Vegas (in other words, the setup for *The Hangover 3*)—but it turned out to be a great weekend of hearing one another's stories and really getting down to the issues with each member of the group.

Las Vegas has plenty of hotels, especially hotels with large suites that could accommodate a bunch of fellas like us, so that was a no-brainer. We got a big room, ordered in some food and drinks, greeted one another, and dove into story time. Things got even crazier when the hotel upgraded us to a suite on the sixtieth floor that had a Jacuzzi tub out on the balcony.

If you can't be honest with others while sitting in a hot tub some six hundred feet in the air and as part of the Las Vegas skyline, then you need help. It's a great way to tear down walls and get into the meat of your story.

I cannot tell you how far this weekend went toward opening up an honest dialogue among all the guys in this group. Being able to hear the details behind each of those guys' stories was eye-opening and refreshing. I had been friends with some of these men for years and found out things about them I'd never known, secrets they'd kept to themselves or just those random childhood moments that are stored in your brain but that you hardly ever think about until you're prodded by some outside source.

We heard it all: what kind of home everyone had grown up in, what kinds of people our parents were back when we were kids and what kinds of people they are now, what our social lives had been like through childhood and adolescence and on into adulthood, how we met our wives, the births of our kids, our outside interests, what sorts of struggles we had back then and what sorts of struggles we were dealing with now . . . you name it, we covered it. If it could be a part of our story, whether a major plot point or a minor derivation, it came out.

And that's how we started to achieve true, life-changing honesty in our group. We were all willing to be so raw with one another, to share our stories in detail—flaws and faults and failures included—and in turn hear one another's stories free of reservation and judgment. And because of that willingness to talk and listen, our group grew in ways we hadn't expected.

We only did that weekend once, though I'd love to do it again, and I'm sure the rest of the guys feel the same way. But while it would be fun to get together for another round of story swapping, we only needed that time once. Yes, some of us have gotten together to hang out since then, but we haven't put together another all-in group weekend like that. It accomplished everything we needed it to do, and all in two short days.

Our first accountability phone call after that weekend was a real joy, and the ways we'd grown closer to one another were palpable, both in the written answers we gave to the questions the night before and in the tones of our voices when we dialed in to the conference call the next day. Everything was more immediate, more raw, more real.

More honest.

And that honesty is what has led us to become the stronger, healthier, more reliable people we are today.

But honesty is not the only thing that accountability takes. There's also another quality that goes hand-in-hand with honesty, and that's courage. It's a subject we turn to in the next chapter.

Chapter 6

YOU NEED COURAGE

*I*n addition to gut-level honesty, true accountability requires something that, deep down, most of us have: courage. This is the real crux of the thing, the enormously hot furnace where all the impurities rises to the surface.

While honesty is basically providing an inventory of who you are, courage is taking a look at that inventory and asking a single, solitary question:

Why?

Why do you do the things you do? Why are you driven to act in a certain way? What obstacles or roadblocks get in your way and keep you from living a life full of freedom?

Imagine this fuller, more accountable life as an adventure. But in order to live this adventure, you're going to have to walk down some untested roads and maybe duck your head into a dark cavern or two that holds nothing but foreboding. Think of any fantastical, quest-type tale you've ever heard or read or seen in a movie, and there is always the inevitable part where the hero must venture into the unknown in order to vanquish the foe.

It's just part of the package. And it takes courage.

Superhero Courage

There's a reason our culture has suddenly been swimming in stories about superheroes—we love courage. We love to see the downtrodden, the runt of the litter, the little guy become the hero, even though it's almost always by accident. We love to see the mild Peter Parker turn into the web-slinging Spider-Man, or the meek Clark Kent remove his glasses and soar through the air as Superman, or even the cocky billionaire Tony Stark learn some lessons about love and friendship as he dons his high-tech suit of armor and becomes Iron Man.

All these characters, whether they embrace their super-powers willingly (Spider-Man, Captain America) or reluctantly (the Hulk, Ben Grimm [aka "The Thing" from *The Fantastic Four*]), they all wind up finding deeper reserves of courage than they previously thought possible.

We all can relate. We all want to feel like we could be

superheroes, if only we could get exposed to gamma radiation or have super-soldier serum injected into our veins. And then we could unlock the vast stores of courage we never seem to be able to tap into.

The thing is: accountability allows for just that very thing. When we get accountable, we open up avenues of courageous, superhero-like behavior. Or possibly even beyond that because, while superheroes tend to fight against city-destroying super-villains bent on world domination, we have to fight against something even more difficult—ourselves.

So where can we find that courage? Because no matter how physically strong some of us may be, the fact of the matter is that we don't have superpowers, and besides, our physical strength isn't going to be any help anyway.

We find courage in the very place where it is required: accountability. Because when we begin to let our accountability partners into our lives, we begin to forge a bond of trust, and along with that trust comes the courage we need in order to ask the tough questions and stare unflinchingly at the answers. We can have courage because we have a team of people supporting us when we look into the scary places of our lives, just as we support them in doing the same thing.

Courage under Fire

We talked about this a bit in the previous chapter, but honesty will only take you so far if you don't have courage—on both sides of the accountability relationship. Asking the tough questions takes courage, even when you've been given the go-ahead to do just that.

It's one thing for your friend to tell you, "Hey, I need you to ask me these tough questions about the deepest, most intimate parts of my life," and another for you to actually do it. Trust me. You can agree in principle all you want to being the bad guy who holds your friend's feet to the fire, but sometimes, when the rubber meets the road and it's time to actually ask those tough questions, it becomes easier to chicken out. To pretend that everything's okay and there's no need to go there.

It takes courage to ask the question.

It takes courage to let the question be asked.

It takes courage to answer honestly.

It takes courage to listen to the answer.

It's really easy to hear a crazy-tough, crazy-intimate question like, "Did you masturbate at all this week?" and blow it off with a confident, "Nope!" And of course, that answer contains an unspoken, *So we can move on to the easier questions now, please!* We can hear the hard questions and immediately turn into those comedic police officers that filmmakers include in their movies, the ones who stand just outside the barrier marked out with the POLICE LINE, DO NOT CROSS yellow tape and who say, "There's nothing to see here. Move along."

That's the easy thing to do. The courageous thing is to answer honestly and admit to your actions, whatever they may be, but especially if the correct answer is "yes."

Honesty is an outlook, a mind-set, a point of view. Courage

is the heart that puts meat on the bones of honesty and enacts it in the real world. You can't have true honesty without courage.

But courage isn't something you can just talk about; it isn't all attitude and swagger, or something you can pull off if you have the right hair stylist or designer pair of shoes. Courage is something you have to put into action, or else it's just words and good intentions.

Courage in Love

The thing about courage is that it is generally intertwined with another of life's great motivators: love. If you are in an accountability relationship or are considering starting one, presumably it's going to be with someone you care about—probably not in a romantic way, but someone you want to see succeed in life and who in turn wants to see you succeed. Someone who cares enough to pour themselves into you and who is close enough to hear and receive all you have to say.

Someone you love.

So what does that love look like? Does it look like giving your accountability partner a pass when they screw up? Does it look like glossing over things when they get uncomfortable in the hopes that they'll just go away on their own?

Or does it look like calling people on their BS whenever they try to pass it off on you? Does it look like checking your gut and owning up to your faults and flaws? Because the fact of the matter is that we're all flawed, and none of us is even remotely close to being perfect, either in our past or in our future. When you try to pretend that everything's great when it isn't, you are just making yourself look bad and could be revealing a huge lack of courage on your part.

Now, I understand that some of us have deeply psychological reasons for holding back or for letting our internal vulnerabilities keep us from being outwardly vulnerable. Some of us have endured far more hardship or abuse than any person should ever rightfully endure, and that keeps us pretending or hoping to skirt past the pain and maintain some semblance of normalcy.

But ignoring the tough stuff doesn't make it go away. It just allows it to fester. Maybe you need to start dealing with the scary stuff, and maybe you need the help of a professional counselor to do that. Maybe you have pain from your childhood that you've buried or locked away, something you need to deal with. Please do. Don't let that stuff control you any longer.

Courage Avoided

It takes courage to stand up for the right thing and to hold people accountable. One example that springs immediately to mind is the terrible, horrible tragedy of all the children whose lives were irrevocably ruined by former Penn State University assistant football coach Jerry Sandusky.

There's probably very little chance that you don't already know at least some of the stomach-churning details of this horrific case, and I'm not going to go into the whole thing because the details of Sandusky's actions are not the point I'm trying to make. He was convicted by a jury of forty-five counts of child sexual molestation and is now serving his sentence, and rightfully so.

The major thing with Jerry Sandusky is that he was given way too much leeway with young boys, whom he would invite onto the Penn State campus through his nonprofit organization called the Second Mile. This organization worked with underprivileged boys in their preteen or early teen years, many of them boys who were being bounced around the foster system, to help them have a sense of belonging and family, a place in this world. Perhaps that very mission is what made Sandusky's alleged actions so egregious, that he would trade on the good work being done by his charity to prey sexually on these underage boys.

Again, though, I'm not wanting to talk about Sandusky's behavior here. That's been rightfully excoriated in plenty of media outlets, and I join in the chorus of condemning each and every one of the heinous acts he was convicted of committing. But what I want to talk about is the complete and utter lack of courage showed by those around Sandusky, both those in authority over him and those who were under his authority.

Several people had the opportunity to put a stop to what was occurring between Sandusky and his victims, and no one did anything.

That is a mind-blowing, jaw-dropping lack of courage.

Eventually, the story came to light when the mother of one

of the abused boys became suspicious and reported it to authorities, which led to a grand jury investigation. It didn't become news because no one at the university did anything—it was only years after the fact that anyone had the courage to step up and speak out about what was clearly criminal behavior.

And it was only after the news came forward and the public outrage began in earnest that Penn State University did anything about it. Soon after the news broke, legendary Penn State head football coach Joe Paterno was summarily fired for his role in allowing Sandusky's actions to occur under his watch. There was a feeling among the higher-ups at the university that Paterno had not acted courageously by censuring Sandusky, though it was unknown at the time how much Paterno really knew about what was going on in the offices and football facilities at Penn State. Unfortunately, Joe Paterno died shortly after his termination, so he'll never be able to speak to the allegations against his program or the Sandusky verdict itself.

The way that the university's leadership handled Sandusky's behavior was the subject of an internal investigation of Penn State by Louis Freeh, a former director of the Federal Bureau of Investigation, who eventually released a 267-page report lambasting the university itself and four men in leadership at Penn State at the time: former president Graham Spanier, former university vice president Gary Schultz, the deceased and ousted former head football coach Joe Paterno, and athletic director Tim Curley, who had been placed on leave.

According to the report, these four Penn State officials exhibited a "total disregard for the safety and welfare" of

Sandusky's victims. To quote from the report: "The most powerful men at Penn State failed to take any steps for 14 years to protect the children who Sandusky victimized." Additionally, the report condemns Spanier, Schultz, Paterno, and Curley as never demonstrating "through actions or words any concern for the safety and well-being of Sandusky's victims until after Sandusky's arrest."[1]

The report also indicates that there was "a critical written correspondence" that addressed another incident of a sexual nature that occurred between Sandusky and a young boy approximately ten years old that was witnessed by a football assistant named Mike McQueary. After seeing this incident, McQueary reported it to his bosses, but according to the written correspondence referred to in the report, neither the incident itself nor McQueary's account of it were ever reported to the proper authorities.

But it was more than oversight—it was a deliberate action, according to this report. The four men had created a plan to report the incident but after talking it over among themselves decided against it. The report, once more, reads, "Their failure to protect . . . the child victim, or make attempts to identify him, created a dangerous situation for other unknown, unsuspecting young boys who were lured to the Penn State campus and football games by Sandusky and repeatedly victimized by him." Further, it states, "Although concern to treat the child abuser humanely was expressly stated, no such sentiments were ever expressed by them for Sandusky's victims."[2]

And if that wasn't bad enough, here's the ultimate kicker—the greatest, most galling instance: this report flatly states that Spanier, Paterno, Schultz, and Curley acted this way "in order to avoid the consequences of bad publicity."[3]

Ironically, the university was sanctioned by the NCAA and was forced to vacate more than one hundred victories that they won during the time frame of Sandusky's crimes. All that effort to cover things up and ensure wins, and all they did in the end was ruin the lives of many young boys and leave their reputations in tatters forever.

Courage is always—always—worth it.

Courage in the Small Things

Yes, this is an extreme example of lack of courage because we all like to think we'd be the type of people who would exhibit the appropriate courage in a situation like this, that we'd be the type of people who would step in and stop something so despicable.

I'm sure all those people who didn't do just that felt the same way at some point.

The fact of the matter is, courage isn't necessarily something we can turn on and off at will. We have to be courageous in the small things to set the stage for being courageous when it counts. Every time we exhibit even the tiniest amount of courage in an accountability setting, we're laying groundwork to show even more courage in larger settings that we don't necessarily anticipate.

Courage and honesty are two sides of the same coin, going hand in hand to create something truly great.

Courage in My Group

After our Vegas get-together, my now regularly scheduled accountability group got much, much closer. We were suddenly way more comfortable with one another (though we'd already been mostly comfortable) and were, on the whole, willing to be more detailed when describing our struggles and triumphs with one another. In short, we grew together as a group.

We began to display more and more courage toward one another in our weekly meetings, so I thought it was time to go even deeper into the particular questions we would ask and answer.

Right around this time, I spoke at a marriage conference (it was one of the gazillion things on that schedule I was trying to tame, the overly crammed calendar that had led to the creation of the group in the first place). While I was at that conference, I heard an interesting fact about the relationship between happiness in a marriage and the amount of times the husband and wife in that couple were engaging in sexual activity. In other words, the more frequently husbands and wives have sex with each other, the happier they are with their marriage. (A good target, by the way, is to have sex with your spouse at least twice a week. The longer men go without sex, the more desperate they become, and the longer women go without sex, the more they don't need it.)

Sadly, the flip side of that is something else I learned at this marriage conference: there is a shocking number of married couples who aren't having very frequent sex. They are taking this critical component of marriage and sidelining it, for whatever reason. For some it's a heart issue (there are problems in the marriage and one or both partners are withholding sex for an emotional reason). For some it's a time issue (one or more of them spends a lot of time away from home for work purposes or something, so the amount of time they have together is limited), for others it's a schedule issue (both of them are too busy and wind up tired every night), and for others it's an opportunity issue (both of them are willing but something—kids, illness, etc.—keeps getting in the way).

Regardless, I was in an accountability group with a bunch of married men. We were about eighteen months into this group at this point, and since we'd all recently experienced a breakthrough in our relationship together, I thought it would be a good idea to test that depth of relationship and ask a courageous question with the hopes of getting courageous answers. So one day I was leading the meeting (I'd been the last caller the week before—even though I put the group together, I was not above the rules), and I decided now was the time and threw out this little conversation starter:

"When was the last time you had sex with your wife?"

At first, it was so quiet that I thought something had gone wrong with the phone lines or that my phone had accidentally dropped the call. I had to take it away from my ear and look at the screen to make sure I was still connected to the call.

Every single one of those guys knew I wasn't looking for locker-room talk, nor was I seeking advice or soliciting ideas on stuff I could take into my own bedroom. I asked this question out of a legitimate concern for my friends' marriages; this was the serious, gut-wrenching, courageous work that an accountability group is supposed to be engaged in.

We were a tight group, but we'd never gone there.

Hence the cricket-chirping silence.

Finally, one of the guys chimed in, quietly and disappointedly, "Actually, it's been about three months." No one said anything, so he continued, sounding like a man with a broken heart, "There have been some issues between us, and I'm not proud of it, but whatever. There you go."

Courage.

You know what the rest of us did? We thanked him for sharing. In fact, another of the guys said, "Thanks for sharing that, man. On my end, it's been about a month." Because the first guy had enough courage to speak out, it gave the second guy enough courage to do the same thing.

That day's conversation changed our group, altering our dynamic for the better. Even though our group was already pretty courageous, that conversation added even more courage to the equation.

Courage begets courage. When you start walking in courage, it becomes even easier to continue doing it, and doing it with more courage.

Now, I'm not talking about recklessness here. You have to include wisdom with your courageousness; otherwise, you're going to take unnecessary risks or, once more, turn into one of those provocateurs who say crazy stuff just to get a reaction out of people, not because you're trying to help but because you're trying to provoke. That isn't courage—that's just stirring the pot.

I'm talking about seeing a need and meeting it with true honesty and integrity. That's the essence of the type of courage we need in our accountability relationships. And it's the essence of what happened next in our group.

I even went so far as to add it to our online list of questions to make sure it kept getting asked and answered. Needless to say, over the next few weeks, our relationships with our wives got stronger—and happier. And it all came about as a result of courage.

Oh, and one quick coda to that whole story: on the first week I asked the question, when one of the guys answered "three months," I called that guy directly as soon as our meeting was over and asked him whether there was anything I could do to help him out. We talked for a little while about what was going on in his life, what obstacles were standing in the way of his relationship with his wife, and what he individually and they as a couple could do to remove those. It was a good conversation that ended up with a lot of consistent prayer, and I'm glad to say that as a result of that day's talks, his marriage began to see a breakthrough. All because he had the courage to answer honestly.

This guy and I began to talk on our own, and he asked me to challenge him relentlessly on this topic of sex with his wife. At the time, they were ten years into their marriage, and it was still a battle that was defeating them both. He needed someone to walk with him through that issue, just not all the guys in our group. I turned out to be that someone, and I committed to helping him change himself—and his marriage—for the better.

That actually leads to another point about what accountability takes, and that's something we'll look at more closely in the next chapter. What is that something? It takes each other.

Chapter 7

YOU NEED HELP

I really hope you didn't find this book listed in the "self-help" section of your bookstore or Amazon, because this whole concept of accountability goes far beyond helping yourself. In fact, the notion of "self-help" flies in the face of accountability.

Because to get accountable you need the help of other people, not yourself.

As the saying goes (and like I remarked earlier), no one is an island, and if the several thousand stories our collective culture has about people on islands hold any truth, it's that we need one another to get through this life.

Throw a dart at your local television listings and you'll find a story that reiterates this truth. Watch just about any family film and you'll hear this same message. Pull a random book from the shelf of your local bookstore and the chances are good you'll be able to pull the "I need assistance" lesson from it.

The point is: it is a universally established truth that life was not meant to be a solo performance.

Mutually Beneficial Relationships

I'm a huge fan of music, and even the greatest solo performers have some sort of collaborative effort to make their music happen, whether it's a dedicated backup band or talented songwriters. Rare are the musicians who write, record, distribute, and perform every single note themselves. Can you think of any? Are they any good?

Instead, what leaps to mind for me are artists like the Beatles, whose best songs were joint efforts between John Lennon and Paul McCartney, or U2, who, despite being fronted by the immensely popular Bono, split all their earnings equally five ways (one part each for the four band members and one part for their longtime manager). Each person contributes something to the overall product, creating something that's far bigger than anything any one of them could do on their own.

Think about that. Here's a band with one of the most recognizable front men on the planet, as well as a track record of relevance that has allowed them to make popular music and play to sold-out venues across the world for more than thirty years. If anyone in the music industry has a right to be stuck-up and selfish, it's the members of U2. Yet they all share everything equally, understanding that they each bring their own unique contribution to the music they make, from the vocals to the guitars, from the bass to the drums, and even to the day-in, day-out aspects of managing a band. The musicians in U2 understand that their manager plays an important role in their success, and, while other bands pay their managers somewhere between 10 and 15 percent of their grosses, U2 welcomes him in with an equal share of what each of them makes.

Each of those people contributes something that enriches the experience of being in U2, something that none of the others is capable of bringing to the table. Well, you will not be surprised to learn at this point that the same thing goes with accountability. When you start to rely on others for help—and find them relying on you in turn—you create a life for each of you that's deeper, richer, and more rewarding than something you could've done on your own. Because you're trusting one another in freedom, honesty, and transparency.

And besides—you were not meant to do this on your own.

More and more in the corporate culture, things are getting open. Technology is becoming increasingly open source, where companies invite any and all developers to contribute their thoughts, ideas, and talents to make software better. And at the corporate office level, companies are starting to understand that walled-off offices are counterproductive to getting things done. The new trend in office culture is to open up floor plans and to start letting workers see how everyone else is doing. Not only does that provide extra accountability, but it allows employees to share ideas and workloads with one another, making for a stronger, more viable company.

By opening things up, people are able to help one another, and when we help one another, we make the world a better place.

One more thing: accountability doesn't work if you're only interested in your story and not theirs. This is a mutually beneficial relationship, and if you're only looking at you (or only looking at them), you'll never progress the way you need to become stronger, healthier, and better adjusted.

Ryan and Jake: Accountability in Action

The great thing about accountability is that it allows you and your accountability partners the opportunities to push one another, to spur one another on to a better life. And nowhere is this more evident than in the world of athletics and exercise.

Take my friends Ryan and Jake. Both of these guys are supermen when it comes to working out. As for me: I'm not a runner and am extraordinarily terrible at about any type of exercise, which is why I have questions about my workout habits in our weekly accountability meetings with my group. You name it, I've tried it. P90X? Yep. CrossFit? Of course. Tae Bo?

I still have those VHS tapes in a box in my attic. ThighMaster? Actually, no. Even I have my limits.

Here's how you know I'm for real when I say that I've tried every type of exercise regimen out there: I owned a Bowflex and the Ab Isolator. That's serious proof.

My problem with working out is that I'm not very good at it. I can try all I want to beef up or put on muscle, but it just doesn't happen. I guess I don't have it in my genes or something, so I do my best to stick to cardio, relying on my accountability group to help keep me on track and keep my heart and lungs healthy and active.

Anyway, this is not an illustration about me; it's about my friends Ryan and Jake. Like I said, these guys practically live for working out, and unlike me, they have the body types to put on some muscle and build their endurance. They're the types of guys who run, swim, and bike Ironman triathlons because they think it's fun.

They also do it as a part of Team XXXchurch (which you can find online at teamxxxchurch.com), a loose gathering of elite athletes who race in things like Ironman triathlons, along with other marathons or extreme races, in order to raise awareness of and funds for XXXchurch. If you're crazy like Jake and Ryan, you should look into it and see what you think.

However, in case you don't know or have never heard of these things, Ironman triathlons are the types of competitions you can't just decide on a whim to participate in. These are intense, grueling endurance contests that require extreme amounts of training. Triathletes laugh at marathoners. They chew them up and spit them out. They eat them for breakfast. Tony Stark, the superhero Iron Man, would get annihilated in one of these.

For reference: an Ironman triathlon starts with a brisk swim of two and a half miles. That's the first leg. After that comes a little bike ride over a distance of one hundred and twelve miles. And once you're through warming up, you get to finish it off with an actual marathon. Yeah, that's running, on your own feet, for 26.2 miles (and now you know the meaning of all those bumper stickers that have been cropping up over the last few years with "26.2" printed on them).

So, you have to already be either crazy or strong (or both) to compete in these events, and Jake and Ryan qualify (on both fronts). But, like I said, you can't just decide the night before that you want to swim, bike, and run that distance. You have to train.

But you can't train by running circles in a hamster wheel or by going out for the occasional and inconsistent run or swim or bike ride or something like that—no, it is a must that you train effectively, and the best way to do that is to train alongside someone else. When you do that, you'll push each other to greater heights and longer distances than you would ever do on your own. There's just something about trying to catch and beat the other guy that forces you to push yourself farther and to dig deeper.

Two people are stronger than one, especially when it comes to accountability. But I'll take this even further—it's not enough just to have other people around you; you have to make sure those people can push you.

My friends do not live in the same town, so they do not train with each other. Ryan lives in Arizona, while Jake lives in northern California. Because of their distance disparity, they each have gathered together a group of people with whom they train. Ryan has assembled a group of fellow athletes who are on either side of his skill level or who have different strengths and weaknesses from his own. So while he may be the better runner, there's someone else who is not as good a runner but who is an amazing swimmer. This helps Ryan push himself when it comes time to train for the swimming portion of the Ironman, while Ryan helps his training partners push themselves whenever they hit the treadmill or running path at the park.

Jake, on the other hand, is definitely the strongest, so he trains with people who, while good, are not as good as he is. He is definitely the strongest person in his group. And don't think I'm knocking Jake right now, because if I were training for Ironman triathlons, I'd probably be tempted to do the exact same thing. It feels good to trash the competition week in and week out; it makes you feel better about yourself and your abilities.

So here we have Ryan, always being pushed through effective competition with his training partners, and then we have Jake, always being the one to push others but never really finding the true boundaries of his limits and his capacity. Got it? Good. Because these two are about to meet.

One time Ryan and Jake came to Southern California, where I now reside, for some meetings we were having about our ministry. Since they're both into competing and Ironman triathlons and all that, they decided—I don't remember whose idea it was—to go on a thirteen-mile run together. That's basically half a marathon, and a good way to test each other's athleticism and overall fitness level. Plus, these guys think something like that is buckets of fun. So it was decided: the next morning Ryan and Jake would start their day off with a brisk thirteen-mile trot, because they are insane. I would stay in the hotel room, order room service, and work in my bed while they ran.

They met up the following day, stretched out, and prepared to hit the pavement. Just before they started out on their run, Ryan asked Jake, "How fast do you want to go?"

Jake, confident in his ability, smiled wryly and said, "You set the pace, man." He knew he could hang with Ryan.

Ryan, on the other hand, smiled his own wry smile and said, "Good luck, bro. You're not going to be able to keep up with me."

"We'll see," came Jake's reply.

Of course, at that moment, it was on.

Right at the outset, Ryan sets the pace at about an eight-minute mile. Jake takes it step for step, stride for stride. Mile one, mile two, mile three . . . Jake is right there with Ryan.

Mile four comes along, and Jake fades a step or two but still keeps up the pace that Ryan set. Mile five, mile six, mile seven.

At mile eight, Ryan is still running effortlessly, barely breaking a sweat and still breathing normally, while Jake is gasping and slapping his feet down on the pavement like they are salamis.

But he's keeping up.

Ryan decides to end this and bumps up the pace to about a seven-and-a-half-minute mile. Jake falls back another step or two, but he still sticks with it. Sure, he is feeling intense pain in his side and can't seem to find enough air to force into his oxygen-deprived lungs, but he is determined to stick with Ryan and follow through on his pre-run bravado.

Mile nine comes, then mile ten, then mile eleven. Still Jake keeps up. Ryan is finally reaching his own threshold for lung capacity and is starting to feel it. The fact that the macho and confident Jake is right on his tail, despite his sputtering and gasping, motivates Ryan to keep up the pace for the last stretch.

Mile twelve comes and they start heading uphill. Once they hit that hill, the game is on. They both want to finish as strong as they can, goading each other, wordlessly daring each other to be the guy who gives up. Ryan keeps his speedy gait, and Jake manages to keep up with him. The last mile comes along and Jake starts trying to finish strong, goading Ryan into putting everything he's got into that last little bit.

They finish the way they started, with Ryan leading the way but Jake just two or three steps behind. As soon as they cross their finish line, Jake collapses on the ground, panting and moaning, taking extreme pleasure in the fact that he was able to keep up for all thirteen miles. Ryan crouches in a rest, breathing a little harder than usual but still in control of all his faculties.

After the two of them caught their breath and got their heart rates down, they headed over to a nearby Starbucks for some oatmeal and coffee. (Which doesn't make sense to me. Who wants to guzzle hot coffee and stuff down hot oatmeal after such a grueling run? Presumably they rehydrated themselves first.) They walked in, got their food and drinks, and headed to a table to sit down for a chat.

"Okay, Ryan," Jake said, "how'd you do that?"

Ryan let Jake know about his training situation, how he has surrounded himself with people who constantly push him to get better.

"I wish I had people like that to train with," Jake said.

You know what Ryan's response was? It's awesome. He said, "Then go find them! Stop surrounding yourself with people you can beat. When I started running, I found a woman who is ten years older than me to run with, and she kicked my tail so much that I got better and faster. I hate to swim, mainly because I'm not very good at it, but it's part of the triathlon, so I went to the pool and joined the Master's Swim class, where I get hammered by fat women and old guys. I started swimming with them because they pushed me just like I pushed you in our run this morning. And I'm a much better swimmer now because of it. I still can't beat them, but I don't lose by as much as I used to, so I know I'm making progress and getting better."

I asked Ryan for more details on his workouts, especially with the woman who can run circles around him at the track. He sent me this quote:

I love to go running with her because she kicks my tail, and she talks a bit of smack about it. She does this in multiple areas of her life. Some people might find her intimidating . . . I don't know, but I think she's awesome. Just this last week I asked her to give me a heavy dose of speed work at the track. I want to get faster, and I knew she could help. She granted my request, pushed the throttle down, and challenged me to go! On my last lap, she came alongside me and paced me to a strong and demanding finish.

You know what? It was hard work, but it was also fun and exhilarating. And, of course, it was extremely rewarding to be able to finish like that.

Ryan is the kind of guy who is always looking for a challenge instead of backing away from opportunities, and he leans into it when someone calls him out or challenges him to the next level of competitive excellence.

Ryan loves the help.

To make accountability work, you need that kind of help. You need someone who will push you, who will encourage you, who will come alongside you and encourage you to keep giving your best because you know they're giving their best. There's no way Jake and Ryan would've run those thirteen miles as fast as they did on their own; it was the mutual encouragement (and inherent competitiveness of their personalities) that kept them going and helped them discover—especially Jake—strength and endurance they didn't know were there.

Here's a little coda to that story: Ryan and Jake recently

participated in an Ironman triathlon, and they both finished strong. I followed their progress on my iPad while I watched the NBA Finals on TV, and Ryan finished the race in just over eleven hours, while Jake took thirteen hours to knock it out. Because of his intense training in the Master's Swim class, Ryan finished the swimming portion of the triathlon in an hour and four minutes, which was one of the fastest times (and faster than the overall third-place finisher). All that training paid off.

And one more small thing: Ryan met Jake at the finish line with a cold, refreshing beer, wanting to be the first guy to congratulate him on finishing the race. Talk about support.

Find Help to Get Strong

If you want to get stronger physically, you have to work out with people who are stronger than you, and the same holds true for accountability. If you want a better marriage, don't turn to newlyweds for advice; instead, consider seeking out a couple who've been in a successful marriage for the last thirty years and find out what they do. Emulate them. Let them push you and encourage you.

Yes, we need to have accountability among our peers and friends, and there's a tremendous benefit to meeting with people who have the same interests as you or who are in the same stage of life as you. You can understand each other, where you're each coming from, because you're both coming from the same spot, the same vantage point, the same area. You can look at each other and say those magic words: "I understand because I'm in the same place."

But you can't let your accountability stop there. I'm not saying you have to have someone older in your accountability group, but you have to recognize your own strengths and weaknesses and then find someone who complements those. Someone who pushes you where you're weak and someone you can push where you're strong.

Because we need one another. We need the best—and worst—of one another so that we can become more together than any one of us could achieve individually.

My Group Gets Stronger

One thing that is easy to conflate is this idea of growing stronger when we're pushed by others. If one guy who is better than me pushes me toward becoming stronger, then surely two guys would make me twice as strong. And ten guys would make me ten times stronger. Right?

Not so much. Sometimes the more people you add, the more you dilute your ability to strengthen one another. Especially in accountability, where communication is vitally important.

It's possible for a group to be so big that it actually winds up weakening those within it. We saw this in our own group, which, you may recall, started out with seven guys, plus myself. It was too many for us to rationally push one another, and that bloat started showing fairly early on.

Shortly after we started (I think even before we got together in Las Vegas), we began to see limited participation from a couple of guys, and then they officially started removing themselves from the group. One of the guys came to me and said he didn't have time for it anymore—his schedule was too busy, and he had another group already going that he could focus on.

Another guy came to me and said he was comfortable with doing the e-mail reports every week, but that's all he had time or space for in his life; he didn't want to do the phone call as well. Unfortunately, the way we'd set up the group, we all felt the call was an integral part of it, and our group was not something you could do only halfway, so this guy wound up dropping out completely and seeking accountability elsewhere.

And then there was the guy who called me shortly after I added the question "When was the last time you had sex with your wife?" He flat-out told me he wasn't going to be comfortable with having to answer that question every week. He said, "This group is starting to go places I don't want it to."

Over time, our group has dropped from eight people to four. When it started dwindling, I have to admit I was kind of surprised. Honestly, I thought less of those guys at first, the ones who took themselves out of the group. But the further we've gotten away from their departure, the more I've started to realize that it was ultimately a good thing. With just four people in our group, we're able to get more out of our half-hour on the phone together every week.

Once people started to bring up that the questions were

making them uncomfortable, we as a group had a decision to make. Do we make the questions easier after eighteen months in order to keep people together? But if we did that, then what was the point in meeting in the first place? Or do we make the questions tougher and more focused so that we can strengthen one another? Do we do the accountability question equivalent of Ryan enrolling in that Master's Swim class or seeking out the better runner in order to push him to get stronger and leaner?

We chose the latter, and some people left; but oddly enough, the pruning of our group made us stronger. We've managed to find the right balance of number of people in the group, strengths and weaknesses, and personalities. Now we're each pushing one another on, encouraging one another, running the same race together, and keeping up with one another as brothers.

We're all getting stronger, much stronger than any of us would be on our own.

So how should you wind up doing accountability? Should you do the same things we've been doing, or modify them for yourself, or do something altogether different? What should accountability look like for you? Let's find out.

Part 3

HOW

Convinced?
Here's how to make it happen . . .

Chapter 8

GET INVOLVED

*R*elationships are tricky. Or, more specifically, the way we allow our relationships to influence us can be tricky. It's easy to look at the diverse array of people in our lives and assign them some measure of equality. A loved one we hold in high esteem can tell us something about ourselves over and over without us ever really hearing it, while a coworker we barely know can mention the same thing and suddenly it sticks.

The thing about accountability is that it requires a two-way relational road. You can't just go pluck your accountability partner (or partners) off the street or hold an online contest where the winner receives a five-dollar Starbucks gift card and an invite into your accountability circle. Nor can you line up all your good friends and casual acquaintances, throw on a blindfold, get spun around a couple of times, and then toss a dart to find that perfect partner.

No, this is a decision that requires a lot of thought and investment, with several factors to consider, including how much history you have with someone, what interests and convictions you have in common, and what stage of life you are in. Let's take a look at some of these factors, with the disclaimer that these are not absolutes—they're more like general guidelines you would do well to follow.

Gender

Narrow your potential list of accountability partners by picking someone who is the same sex as you. Look, I'm all about bridging the gender gap and all that, but the simple fact is that while there are many similarities between men and women, and stereotypes and labels often get in the way of seeing people as they are, men are more comfortable talking about their innermost struggles with other men, and the same holds true for women. It's just the way it is, and we'd all be foolish to ignore our inherent biases and pretend they don't exist.

I'm not saying this is a hard-and-fast, unbreakable rule, but it is a truth for the overwhelming majority of our population. Accountability is not something you do to look good to the world around you—it's something you do in order to live a freer, more well-rounded life, and, as we already mentioned, that's going to require gut-level honesty. You will need to feel comfortable opening up about your deepest, darkest, scariest, most monstrous secrets—the stuff you can barely even admit to feeling or thinking.

Have as many friends of the opposite sex as you want, celebrate them and their general awesomeness, march in parades for them, and defend them to any and all detractors. Yes, those are wonderful things and attributes for you to have. But accountability is tough enough without having to tiptoe around gender issues or to sugarcoat stuff, so do yourself a favor and stick with someone who shares your own gender.

History

It's also a good idea to seek accountability with someone you have at least a little bit of history with. While it's entirely possible to have a great accountability relationship with someone you barely know, you'll be spending a lot of time just getting to know each other. So what happens if you find out you're not really all that compatible, so to speak?

Instead, it's a good idea to partner with someone you already know, someone you feel good about and who in turn feels good about you. It helps if you've already walked a few miles with the person and know their personality. Likes and dislikes. Areas where they struggle and areas where they have no problems at all.

Of course, in my own group, I had a history with each of the people in it, though they didn't necessarily have a history with one another outside of me. As I mentioned, this made it a little awkward at first, but after having that get-to-know-you session in Las Vegas, we all realized we had some of the same history, though we hadn't gone through it together. Again, like I said, these are suggested guidelines, not hard-and-fast rules that were etched in stone by the finger of God and handed down to me by Moses. That's some serious history.

Point of View

Like we talked about earlier, while you don't want a yes-man (or woman) or a choir to preach to, you also don't want someone who doesn't see the world the same way as you. Choose someone who has a lot of the same thoughts and philosophies about life as you but who maybe doesn't believe exactly the same thing about every possible thing. You may disagree about the finer points of politics, for example, but agree on the motivations you have for wanting or needing accountability, and the methods you're using to get there.

The good thing about partnering with someone who has slightly different views from your own is this: you know you're going to be supported in the major things, but when it comes to the smaller things, you may wind up hearing a new opinion or viewpoint articulated and then grow as a result. The last thing any of us should want is to stay the exact same person we are now—we always want to be growing and improving, and we can only do that when we carefully consider what others say, even if their points of view differ from our own.

Trust

Again, like I wrote earlier, the accountability relationship is all about trust. You have to be able to trust the person who is partnering with you for accountability, and they must feel the same way about you. If you know someone who has a problem keeping secrets or if they tend to gossip about others, they are probably not going to be the best person to consider allowing into those deep, sacred parts of your life.

Your accountability partner is a person who will sometimes have to call you out—and whom you will sometimes have to call out. This relationship isn't just about being nice and providing a listening ear or a shoulder to cry on, though it does contain those attributes. No, it's also about holding each other to a certain standard of behavior. That requires an immense amount of trust, and trust isn't something you can manufacture with a stranger.

Stage of Life

Here's a factor to consider that I don't have a direct answer for: the stage of life. When I say "stage of life," I'm talking about things like income, age, marital status, and kids. Do you want to partner with someone who is at the same stage of life as you, who has all the same pop-culture touchstones from child-hood, and who understands the pressures of raising a family and making ends meet because they're feeling those pressures at the same time as you? Or do you want someone who has already been through those things and can therefore offer the wisdom of experience?

I don't know. It all really depends on what you want to get out of the relationship—and what you want to put in. Maybe you're the one with all the wisdom and you're looking for someone to share it with. Maybe you are just embarking on adulthood and are looking for someone to help you figure it out. Or maybe you are still in the throes of adolescence and need someone like yourself to talk to.

I can't tell you how you need to make this particular deci-sion, because it's really up to what you feel you need. I can, however, reiterate: if you want to get stronger, you have to train with people who will push you, and nowhere will you need to be pushed more than here, in this "stage of life" arena.

My friend Ryan, the triathlon competitor, put it this way: "Sometimes when you're on the bike, you don't know how slow you are riding until someone blows your doors off. At that point, you have two options: you can either ride a lot harder, or you can get left in the dust." Someone who is in the same stage of life as you can help you ride harder, or you can help them ride harder, as you continually "blow the doors off" each other.

Once more, I can't tell you how to play out this concept

of stage of life in your own accountability walk, but it is something to keep in mind, an extra factor in your decisions as you start out on the journey to accountability.

Not a Small Group

While we're here, let's talk about something else to make sure we're all on the same page: your accountability group is not the same thing as a small group. For those of you who are churchgoers, you'll understand that terminology of "small group" right away. If you aren't fluent in church jargon, though, let me translate it.

Many churches, especially evangelical ones, encourage small group gatherings outside of the regular Sunday morning service, meeting in different homes belonging to the congregants. Small groups are usually made up of a handful of couples or families, and the point is to make intentional connections within the church so you have a group of people to walk through life with.

Sounds a lot like accountability, right? But there's a big difference because small groups—or at least the ones I've seen from the outside or the one I was a part of—tend to revolve around some interesting conversation that more often than not includes holding forth on the pastor's most recent sermon or a book you're all reading together. Talking about the lack of sex in your marriage or how you're lying on your taxes . . . well, those topics tend to not come up much.

I was once in a small group, and though I can see how they would be beneficial in certain respects, I overall am not a fan, mainly because I think a lot of churches do it wrong, putting the focus on the wrong things.

Sometimes they sacrifice depth for variety, which actually happened to a friend of mine. He and his wife were involved in a small group for two and a half years, and it had become a real life-giving source of community for them, a rare place where they could go deep with one another. But they had to start meeting outside of the church bounds. Why? Because the church decided to kill their small group and change the way the entire church's small group ministry was structured, putting everyone into new small groups every eight weeks. Musical chairs meets musical small groups. After eight weeks, the small group members would move on to another group. The intent was to allow people to meet all sorts of other new people, but that intent backfired because as soon as they would start to get comfortable meeting together, they would be on to another group.

Anyway, that particular rant against church stupidity aside, my wife and I did once decide to join a small group. It was a few years ago, when we attended a church pastored by my friend Bryan. We lived close to each other, and when the church started implementing and promoting small groups for its members, my wife and I decided to co-lead one with Bryan and his wife. The big upshot was that the church was going to provide a babysitter, and our son and their son were the same age and the best of friends, so it meant they would get to hang out together while we parents were hanging out together.

Not a bad deal, eh?

But it got even better because when we got together for our first week of our new small group, no one showed up except the four of us, our kids, and the babysitter. Bryan was the lead pastor, and I was the porn pastor, so no one wanted to be in a small group with us. Who would want to join that group? That would be like being in a small group with the principal of your high school and that one weird kid at every school who says crazy things and makes everyone uncomfortable.

We didn't care, though. We thought we'd scored big time: a babysitter for the kids and no other priorities.

We went out to dinner and had a great time.

Most weeks, that was the way it went. We occasionally had someone else show up, but as soon as they discovered who was leading the group, they found another place to be the following week.

So it became this awesome time we could look forward to every Tuesday night, a time when we could pretend to have a small group but instead wound up hanging out as a couple of families. We got to know one another even better than we already did, and our families got very close—and still are to this day. We cared for one another, opened up to one another, and wound up accomplishing more in each of our lives and our overall outlook than we ever would have if we'd actually had a small group with more than just us.

The bummer here is that our families are both so busy that

something like this probably would never have happened on its own. We would most likely never have organized regular family get-togethers without the context and pretense of the small group through our church. We would never have said on our own, "Hey, what if we meet for dinner as two families every Tuesday night?" But because we called it a small group, that led us to something, and that something turned out to be great.

And I guess that points out something important, a thread that runs throughout accountability, which is that it's really all about connection and community. But unlike small groups, where connection and community are enough, accountability also calls for action, for change, for a deeper outcome than you would obtain in your ordinary small group.

Getting Motivated

My friend Ryan Russell, the leadership developer I mentioned earlier (as well as the Ryan of the "Ryan and Jake run thirteen miles" story), wrote this great blog post about motivation on his leadership blog (which is called, once more, RedBikeLeader .com). With his permission, I've reprinted it here:

My motivation comes from attaining the next step.

Bumping up to the next level.

Reaching just beyond where I currently am.

Perhaps most of us get defeated by the bigness of a great dream so we never begin. A great realization for most of us could be: You don't have to be the best as long as you can keep striving to improve.

I never imagined running a marathon when I first laced up my shoes. In fact, it wasn't even on my list of goals at that point. My first training run (just over two years ago) was two grueling miles near my house. Those same two miles haunted me for six months. I began to hate those city blocks. But each time I went out, I wanted just to get a little bit better.

Now I use the same approach with everything: writing, reading, coaching, health, leadership, weight loss . . .[1]

It's true. There's something about reaching even the smallest level of success that motivates you to try for more. Think of a toddler climbing up a set of stairs and how absolutely enormous that staircase must look to them. But toddlers don't have the capacity to get overwhelmed by the length and height of a staircase, nor by how steep it is or how many stairs it has. They just focus on getting up to the next step.

Whatever goal you're trying to achieve, whether it's financial independence or shedding a certain number of pounds or cleaning the house, it's good to set a big goal but then figure out all the little steps you need to take to make it happen. You can't just look at the top of the staircase and wish yourself up to the top of it; sooner or later, you have to start climbing. And once you get up one step, you'll find more confidence to get to the next one and then to the next one. And soon you'll look back and see how far you've come, and you'll find that motivates you to get to the next step and the step beyond that one.

And you keep climbing and climbing and doing all you can and focusing both on your long-term goal and on the small steps, and before you know it, you're at the top.

You did it.

You got motivated.

And nothing will ever be the same again.

My Group: Similarities and Differences

In the case of my own group, we have a good balance of friendship, history, point of view, and stage of life. When I set it up, I did so to include only men, so that answers the gender question. And as far as trusting one another, we stepped ahead light-years when we gathered together in Las Vegas for our weekend of sharing and listening.

We have a really good dynamic within our group of people who can push one another in encouraging ways and come alongside one another when we need it. But none of us is a carbon copy of the other; we all have our own beliefs on diverse topics like politics or parenting, on fashion or the finer points of theology.

We have enough differences—strengths and weaknesses—to bring our unique viewpoints to the conversation, but enough similarities to be able to approach one another with familiarity, to throw our arms around one another and say, "Me too, man. Me too."

While I was working on this book, I came across an

interesting bit of research, a study by a couple of researchers at the University of Toronto and at James Madison University (in Harrisonburg, Virginia). The study, provocatively called "Cognitive Sophistication Does Not Attenuate the Bias Blind Spot," asserts—effectively proves—something we already know instinctively: we give ourselves far more leeway for our actions than we grant to others.

Writing about this study in the *New Yorker*, Jonah Lehrer suggests that

> the bias blind spot arises because of a mismatch between how we evaluate others and how we evaluate ourselves. When considering the irrational choices of a stranger, for instance, we are forced to rely on behavioral information; we see their biases from the outside, which allows us to glimpse their systematic thinking errors. However, when assessing our own bad choices, we tend to engage in elaborate introspection. We scrutinize our motivations and search for relevant reasons; we lament our mistakes to therapists and ruminate on the beliefs that led us astray.[2]

Carrying this thought further, Lehrer concludes that our biases "are largely unconscious, which means they remain invisible to self-analysis and impermeable to intelligence."[3]

In other words, we make excuses for ourselves while we simultaneously fillet those around us. We do this because we know exactly where we're coming from while remaining in the dark about where they're coming from.

Being in an accountability group helps mitigate this inherent bias toward ourselves. When we put together the right kind of group, we give each person in that group—whether it's one close friend or a tight-knit collaboration of people—the keys to our biases. We give them the opportunity to hold up a mirror to our behavior and show us what we look like to the rest of the world.

We get to see what we're like to those who aren't doing the same mental processing we're doing. Who aren't leaping through the same internal hoops, connecting the same dots in our minds, tasks that we do completely subconsciously and without realizing what we're even doing.

That's why it's so important to have the right people helping you stay accountable and who you in turn are helping to stay accountable. They're going to have to interpret your actions, your words, your motivations—and you'll have to do the same for them—so you want people who will approach that task completely unafraid and with full awareness of the need for grace, respect, love, honesty, and courage.

Accountability Is Stronger When Smaller

On the flip side of things, you have to remember that there's only so much you can do. It's not your job to keep everyone in the world accountable—that's the whole reason I initially limited our group to only eight people, and why we got stronger once we pared it down to four. In an accountability situation, the group dynamic has to be small enough so that you can listen well, giving everyone a chance to say what they need to say without feeling rushed or trampled upon. And that includes yourself. Because it'll eventually be your turn to talk, you want to be the type of listener you would want to talk to.

I think one thing that has really helped in our group is that we've become friends. Like I mentioned earlier, everyone started off as my friend, but not everyone knew everyone else. Over time, especially after that weekend in Las Vegas, each guy in my group has become friends with each other guy in my group, to the point where I no longer have to be the mediator between friends. These guys—who didn't even know one another when we started not that long ago—are now calling one another every week, connecting over the phone, meeting for coffee, hanging out, seeing movies together, introducing their families to one another's families . . . it's become a real friendship.

It's more than just asking and answering questions now. It's deeper than that. Stronger.

We know we're committed to one another now, no matter what may come down the road. And we're committed to putting in the work and effort that accountability takes. Because make no mistake, accountability does require work and effort—on all fronts, from each member of the group, in both speaking and listening. It isn't something you can glide through and still truly respect the process or the people in your group. But when you put in that work and effort, you'll find how rewarding it can be.

Sure, we may not wind up voting for the same candidate in the next election, but that doesn't matter. We're too busy focused on the eternal stuff, on the meat and potatoes of our lives, to worry about being divided over something ultimately so small.

Chapter 9

GET INTIMATE

In May 2011, Antonio Cromartie, a cornerback for the New York Jets of the National Football League, was out of town when he received a disturbing text message from his wife. In the message, Cromartie's wife told him that she had just cut her wrists and taken a handful of some pills in an effort to kill herself. Distraught, Cromartie called the police in his hometown in New Jersey and told them his wife had just tried to commit suicide. The dispatcher sent some officers to the Cromartie residence. They knocked on the door and, failing to get a response and expecting the worst, took an ax and a sledgehammer to it, forcing their way inside.

The police officers did indeed find Cromartie's wife in the house, but instead of bleeding to death, she was sleeping in her bed, cuddled up with her two daughters.

Turns out she hadn't tried to commit suicide at all. Instead, she suspected that Cromartie—who has fathered many children with multiple women—was cheating on her and mistakenly thought that sending him text messages indicating that she had attempted suicide would help him stay faithful.

This is the opposite of accountability.

But this unusual story does give us something to think about. Namely, what about our spouses? Where on the accountability curve do they fall? What is their role when it comes to your accountability, and what is your role when it comes to theirs?

What Are You Seeking Accountability For?

For starters, it all depends on what you're seeking accountability for. Trying to clean up your diet or stick to that exercise regimen? Then it's probably a good idea to include your spouse—and even the rest of your family—in the loop to support and encourage you as you take these positive steps, or even come along on the ride with you and curtail their own dietary choices to line up with yours. (After all, it's tough to eat a salad for dinner when everyone else is chowing down on pepperoni pizza.)

But what if you're working on your porn addiction or your compulsion to read erotic novels on your e-book reader? What if you're trying to get accountable because you have a wretched thought life or you tend to indulge in fantasies? What if the thing you're trying to change about yourself involves something of an intimate nature? What do you do then?

This is a tough one because a good marriage is one where you don't have to keep secrets from each other. I think most husbands and wives want to have the type of relationship where they feel like they could say or admit to anything and still feel loved and accepted while still understanding that their behavior might not necessarily be condoned. You want to feel like you could look your wife in the eye and say, "Yes, I was ogling that woman wearing the yoga pants in the grocery store" or look your husband in the eye and say, "Yes, I did fantasize about the hunky college student who put in our landscaping."

But the cold reality of it is this: We do not always think this way. Because we are so very intimate with our spouses—connecting with each other at our rawest times physically, emotionally, and spiritually—it can sometimes feel like a form of rejection to hear them admit to expressing interest in anyone but us. We would like to be an all-accepting, always-understanding person, but we can't always be, because it hurts our feelings.

So what do you do? Ultimately, this is a decision you'll need to make for yourselves because only you and your spouse can decide how much of your husband's or wife's inner dialogue you can handle. That's going to be different for each of you. But you and your spouse must come to an agreement that you both support, because that's what marriage is all about.

If you both feel like you can handle being each other's accountability partners, then by all means go for it. Who better to run life's race with? But I've found that this is extremely rare among couples. In most cases, it's good to have an outside person to help hold you accountable, someone who is unencumbered by all the other decisions and considerations that come with marriage, things like parenting techniques and finances. You and your spouse already have many other challenges facing you and many other decisions you must make together. It only makes sense to seek some outside accountability, if only because that outside person can take a bigger-picture view with you and help you see things that your spouse—who is there in the trenches right along with you—might miss.

How Much Do You Tell Your Spouse?

So let's assume you are like the vast majority of people in an accountability relationship and you're meeting regularly with someone of your same gender who is not your spouse. Great! Congratulations.

How much do you share with your husband or wife when you get home? Nothing? Is it like some big secret society meeting that they are allowed to know absolutely zero about? Or can you give them the gist of what you talked about? Should you give them the gist of what you talked about?

Again, this is the type of thing you and your spouse need to figure out in order to come to a place of total agreement—where you're both pleased at the outcome. If you feel like your husband needs to know what you talked about at your meeting and he agrees that he's capable of hearing that without judgment or retaliation, then by all means, speak away. If you believe your wife needs to hear the confession you just made to your accountability partner and that she is on the same page and will listen without confrontation, then you are welcome to say your piece.

The main thing is that you both agree on what should and should not be said, and that agreement comes from a healthy place of mutual trust, not passive-aggressive manipulation or outright bullying. If that's the case, then you have larger issues between the two of you and should seek out ways to remedy or repair those.

And this should really go without saying, but I'm going to say it anyway: your accountability partners' business is between you and them, and whatever's going on with them is something that stays between you and them. They must be able to trust that you will not divulge any of their raw, precious, intimate secrets to anyone. If they wanted your spouse to know their business, then they would tell your spouse their business. That's not your job.

A Trustworthy Spouse

One of the problems we can encounter when we approach accountability with the wrong mind-set—especially when we do it with our spouse—is when it turns into emotional police work instead of encouragement. We have to have the right heart and approach, or things can go downhill really quickly. If you don't ultimately trust your spouse, or if your spouse doesn't ultimately trust you, then accountability can turn from a place of safety into a place of accusation where you feel like you must defend yourself constantly against the mere thought of impropriety.

I'll give you an example. Now, granted, this is an extreme example, but it is a true story that happened to a friend of mine, and it indicates the depths to which police-style spousal accountability can go. My friend—let's call him "Joseph"—had been struggling with gambling. Since his wife was the person who had been most hurt by his addiction, he kept her aware of his struggles and what he was doing to combat them. She became someone he was accountable to for this issue.

Things were going fine until one day Joseph had temporarily relapsed, and his wife had proof. But she didn't do the loving thing and come to him, asking, "What's going on? What happened here?" Instead, she decided that he needed to be taught a lesson and that she needed to be the one to teach it to him.

Operating entirely out of hurt feelings and not a bit of love or logic, she decided she needed to get back at him, to hurt him the way he'd hurt her. I can guess what you're thinking, and I can tell you that, no, she didn't run out and have an affair or anything like that. Instead, she was more creative; she opened up a handful of credit card accounts under Joseph's name and then proceeded to purchase anything she wanted, using those cards.

When the bills came due, she chucked them in the trash instead of making the payments.

To the credit rating agencies, Joseph quickly became an immense credit risk, a guy who maxed out any credit card he had, who ran up a huge amount of debt and then refused to pay any of it.

That'll show him.

So what happened next? Did Joseph's wife come clean to him? Nope. He didn't find out about this behavior directly from his wife. Instead, he discovered what had happened only when he went to buy a new car and was rejected by the dealership for having terrible credit. Joseph knew that couldn't be true, started digging into his finances, and uncovered the mystery credit card debts. Once he confronted his wife about it, she owned up to her behavior and told him, "At least I got something to show for all my spending."

Now, I tell this story not to try to dictate the way Joseph's wife should've felt in the situation. She felt hurt and betrayed, and she had every right to feel that way. She was not emotionally ready to be Joseph's accountability partner, and as a result, she acted rashly, out of pain and anger instead of love and grace. Please don't think I'm trying to put down this woman or her own emotions.

I'm telling you this story to help you see some of the pitfalls inherent in sharing accountability with your spouse in the hopes that you'll avoid them. If your husband or wife is the type of person who can handle your occasional slip-up, then you're probably on solid ground. It does require, though, the ability to look at oneself objectively to try to preemptively determine how you would react in a given situation. And you and your spouse have to be in communication with each other; meaning you have to be in unity, on the same page emotionally and mentally, if spousal accountability is going to work. It is only through that constant communication and those "same page" discussions that you will find yourselves truly keeping each other accountable.

A Positive Story of Spousal Accountability

Whenever I write a book, I send out the early drafts to a few of my trusted friends and readers and ask them for their input on whether it's any good or not, and the same thing happened with the book you're now holding in your hands (or stored on the e-book reader that you're holding in your hands, as the case may be). One of my trusted readers wrote me back about the story I just included, about my friend Joseph and his wife, and suggested that I include along with it a positive story of accountability in a marriage.

With that in mind, here's something my friend Adam wrote about his own journey to accountability, and the role his wife, Michelle, played in it. As is often the case with the types of stories I'm around as a result of my work with XXXchurch, this one has to do with porn, but I think it can apply to other situations and struggles. You may wind up seeing a little bit of yourself in it.

Here it is.

I had a wonderful, carefree childhood. Most of my memories of the time are centered on the typical things: playing with my friends, jumping my bike off curbs, learning to ride a wheelie, and watching far, far too much television.

I've been thinking a lot lately about one memory in particular, though. When I was about seven years old, I spent the night at my friend Ben's house; the following morning, at Ben's suggestion, we went into the woods behind his house to play. Ben said that adults often went there at night, and they usually left cool stuff behind. It would be like a treasure hunt of sorts.

So Ben and I set out. It was a crisp day, though the grass and trees were brown and dead. We wandered around a bit and found a clearing that had obviously hosted a party the night before. Beer cans were strewn about, and a few bottles. I distinctly remember a small tuft of wiry brown grass covered with cigarette butts and spent pull tabs from aluminum cans.

But even more distinctly, I remember the pages, torn from a magazine. The breeze rustling them, causing them to flap their corners, like they were waving hello, greeting me invitingly.

Pages with pictures.

You know where this is going.

I had no real concept of pornography yet. I knew it was wrong for me to be naked in front of other people and that it was wrong for me to see other people naked. I don't know how I knew this—I don't remember my parents ever talking to me about it, though I do have a dim recollection of some freak-out among one of my folks for some nakedness-related reason.

Standing in that clearing, grasping those glossy pages, I didn't even know the word *pornography*, but I did know what seeing those pictures did inside me. How they generated a seething, roiling, complex tumult of lust, shame, excitement, and guilt.

I knew that I shouldn't be seeing this.

And I also knew that I wanted to see more.

I was a seven-year-old boy, and without asking for it, I'd just gotten addicted to porn.

I don't remember much about the moments that immediately followed. I can't be sure, but I think I folded up a couple of those pages and snuck them home in my pillowcase, and I think my mom found them. If there was fallout from that or some teachable moment that my parents seized, I don't remember it at all. I think that must've happened, though, because I never saw those magazine pages again.

Fast-forward to sixth grade. We'd moved from Texas to Oklahoma, and I had a whole new set of friends. Growing up in a semi-rural town in the buckle of the Bible Belt, I had no shortage of churchgoing friends and classmates, and most of the kids I ran with were pretty good kids. You know how most people have those few people in their childhoods who constantly offered temptation to do something you shouldn't do? I didn't have those kids.

But I did have feelings I couldn't explain or understand. I would periodically be overwhelmed with an urgent desire to see a naked woman. Often I'd dig up a *National Geographic* magazine from the school library and root through it in search of native nudity. Once, I spent about three days craving something to slake my thirst for porn; I got it on a class trip to a pottery manufacturer where I saw a small ceramic statue of a nude woman. I'm sure it was very artistic, but my sense of God's sublime, creative act in designing the female figure had been warped, and now it was just something to consume. Something to feed my hunger.

Adolescence and puberty brought increased awareness of what I was dealing with (though I still had no concept of the far-reaching ramifications), as well as the physical outlet of masturbation, but opportunities to see porn were few and far between. This was the mid-1980s, so there was no Internet yet; porn had to make the rounds in magazines and scrambled pay-per-view cable channels. I had access to only one of those, so when my parents were gone, I would click the TV all the way up to the 50s and gawk at whatever I could make out through all the wavy lines and photonegative colors.

Then there was the time when someone—an acquaintance, not a friend—brought a magazine to school in the eighth grade. After school, a handful of other boys and

I gathered in an alcove outside to marvel at this treasure while we waited for our buses to come pick us up. But being there, using pornography with other people, outdoors, at school . . . it was too uncomfortable to me, so I stepped away. Which is why I didn't get in trouble when the door suddenly popped open and the shop teacher came outside to confiscate the magazine.

Now that I'm writing this, I've just remembered another time. Ninth grade. Band trip. Embassy Suites in Chicago. One of the upperclassmen found a magazine in his hotel room, and word spread like wildfire. It wasn't long before we were all in that room, taking turns with it. There was a movie on the hotel TV that night too. I think every male in concert band watched it, because it became an in-joke among most of us. This became the first—and last—time I ever used pornography around someone else.

All these instances were followed by deep shame and inward rage. I'd let God down; I'd let myself down; I'd let my future wife down. Pornography intertwined itself with my naturally depressive personality to teach me very early on how to feel inadequate and how to pile on myself for missing the mark. I marked all the passages in my Bible about sexual sin and did my best to work hard and not fall anymore.

And you know what? It kinda worked. By diving into schoolwork, friendships, and the standard adolescent pining-after-girls stuff, I was able to derail my urges, and they began to flare up less frequently. I made it through high school and my first couple of years of college, fully embracing an emerging musical side and journeying through a couple of bands. By this time I had cable TV in my bedroom and discovered that Showtime came in pretty well, but I wound up being fairly restrained about how I'd watch it. Yes, I'd mess with their late-night lineup on occasion, but these times were rare.

So I thought I had a handle on it, and, like so many times before, my desire for pornography faded into the background of my life. I met a wonderful girl who became my new best friend, we got married, we started having kids, and our dreams of doing music together were put on hold while I soldiered through corporate America for a little while.

It was around 2000, 2001, when, searching the Internet for a trivial piece of information for a script I was writing, I clicked on a harmless-looking link that had cropped up in my search results. Windows began popping up all over my screen, each one featuring salacious images, each one enticing me to click for more. My computer monitor turned into a rapid-fire shooting gallery as I closed each pop-up advertisement as fast as they came up until there were no more.

But it was too late. I was hooked again.

It was the same thing all over, but this time I wasn't a little boy in the woods with a scrap of magazine in my hand. This time I was a responsible adult with the power and unlimited possibilities of the Internet just a click away.

And that began a two-year descent into full-blown

addiction, with an alarmingly regular cycle of binging and purging. I would use every day for a week, then come to my senses, kick myself, feel like crap, promise never to do it again, then spend the next three weeks working at just being "better" and "trying harder." Always hiding, always covering my tracks. Always worried I'd be found out, that Michelle would wake up or come home early. Always convincing myself I'd be okay with that well-worn phrase that comes straight from the devil's lips: "No one has to know."

Two years. Two long years.

The whole time I always convinced myself that I really could be better, that I could fix this on my own. Of course, that was two years of constant frustration and failure, peppered with occasional bouts of thinking I had a handle on my addiction, and even the additional hubris of convincing myself I'd beaten it.

But time and again I would go back to the poison well. Fall, fail, repeat.

And then came the day. I don't know how I landed on it, but I found an unorthodox website, billed as "The #1 Christian Porn Site," called XXXchurch.com.

Just as I'd stumbled into my addiction, I stumbled into the lifeline that would help pull me out of it.

At the time, XXXchurch's website didn't have a whole lot of features, but it had enough. There were astounding stats about the reach of pornography into our culture, and while those had a major impact on me, what really broke my heart and put my feet on the road to recovery was something called "The Wall." It was nothing more than a message board where people could request help or encourage others to overcome their addiction. I read pages and pages, post after post after post, and the realization literally made me weep.

I was not alone.

I thought I had been the only one with this struggle, the only person this wretched, the only man in the world who was this subservient to his own lust. I certainly didn't know anyone else who had dealt with it or who was currently dealing with it. Pornography was—and still is—the dirty little secret that no one wants to talk about, but many people—more than you know—fight against it on a daily (or hourly, or minute-by-minute) basis.

So that began my turnaround. I say "began" because, concerned more with my image than with my heart, I didn't tell anyone about it. I found a sort-of treatment plan through XXXchurch and embarked on it, convinced that I was now taking real steps to clear this up, remove it from my life, and move forward.

And still, no one would have to know.

That attitude lasted less than a week. The longer I worked at sobriety, the more I knew I would have to tell Michelle eventually. I waited for what seemed the best time (by the way, there's really no great time to confess your porn addiction to your spouse, so *now* becomes your best option), sat Michelle down on the couch, and told her everything.

For me, this is the most painful part of the story. Our story. Raw honesty is often painful, but the truth will always set you free, though it may take its time doing it. I'm not going to write down the exact emotional content of those moments on the couch and the days that followed them, but I will charitably call them "difficult" and let you extrapolate.

Fortunately, I married up, and Michelle's side of this story is hers to tell, and maybe she will one day. But we worked through this—and in some ways are still working through it—and have come out on the other side more deeply in love and stronger in our marriage.

Michelle turned into my biggest encourager and became, over time, a safe place where I could talk about my struggles and temptations. If I am feeling a moment of weakness coming on, I know I can go to her with it and find a sympathetic, understanding ear. She gets my accountability reports, and that knowledge helps me make better decisions online just about every day. My temptations come and go, but she is consistent and will always be there.

And while I'd like to say that since that evening confession just before Valentine's Day in 2003, I've had nothing but continuous victory over my addiction, it wouldn't be even remotely close to the truth. I still struggle from time to time, though not nearly as much as I used to. I learned early on that claiming total defeat over pornography usually leads me to a spell of use, so let's just say that it's been awhile—a long while—since I looked at porn, and I hope to keep it that way. Still, I'm taking it one day at a time, knowing that my wife is my biggest fan and greatest encourager.

Adam's story is one we can all hopefully gain encouragement from, and while his particular struggle is with pornography, I hope you can see your own struggle or temptation in that story. Our bad habits tend to start early in life, and they often seem insurmountable, like Adam says porn was for him. You may not see yourself in the exact content of that story, but I sincerely hope it gives you a vision for what accountability with your spouse—when done right—can look like.

What about the Rest of the Family?

What about your parents? Your kids? Your brothers or sisters? Do they have a right to know what's going on with you? Can they be in an accountability relationship with you?

Again, I'm only proposing guidelines, not hard-and-fast rules; but trying to remain accountable to your own parents or your own kids can get a little dicey. It really depends on the stage of life you're in. My own children are still young, and I want them to feel like they can tell me anything, but I'm not going to open up to them about what I'm going through, simply because they're not old enough to handle it.

Even if your children are adults, the chances are likely that they look to you for wisdom and advice on how best to tackle life, so entering into an accountability relationship—which is essentially a peer-to-peer, back-and-forth, ongoing conversation—is probably not going to be the best idea. However, if you feel like it could be a mutually beneficial relationship, where both you and your child are seeing eye to eye and are mature enough to take hearing each other's business—and to call each other out on mistakes or missteps—then feel free to give it a try. I'm not guaranteeing success, and I'm not too crazy about the thought, but stranger things have happened—and worked.

As for siblings, they can be terrific accountability partners because you definitely share a common background and, most likely, have at least a few mutual interests. Plus, if you and your sibling are both interested in being in an accountability relationship with each other, then you most likely see eye to eye on a lot of things and would likely find it astonishingly easy to hold each other accountable. In fact, there's a decent chance that you are already doing it and just haven't formalized it by calling each other "accountability partners."

Beyond that, I have no real advice for other family members and accountability. Uncles, aunts, siblings-in-law, cousins, grandparents . . . it's all a judgment call for you, based on the level of comfort you both may have with each other and with the rigors and demands of the accountability relationship.

Of course, when you talk about family, sometimes you may find yourself a little surprised. Recently I was at an event that XXXchurch puts on through various churches across the region called "Porn and Pancakes." It's basically a spin on the old "Saturday morning men's breakfast" idea you find in a lot of churches, except instead of getting men together to pray, we talk about the devastating effects of pornography on the people who make it, on the men who use it, and on society in general when it becomes prevalent.

Obviously, when we're putting on these events, one of the big things we talk about is accountability, along with x3Watch. As usual, I gave a little commercial for the software in the midst of my larger talk, and then I had a chance to meet some of the attendees afterward. Two of the people I met were an older man and his teenage son. They introduced themselves, and the dad talked to me at length about x3Watch, about how he thought it was a really great idea, and how he wanted to use it. Then he turned to his son and said, "What do you think about getting that software on our computers?"

The son smiled broadly, gave a chuckle, and said, "Dad, I've already been using it. I do it with my best friend. We've been keeping each other accountable for three years now."

I don't know if that father and son wound up becoming accountability partners or not, but I really dug both of those people. I was impressed that the son was already using it, and I was impressed that the dad was willing to be vulnerable to his son, to show a little bit of his humanity. Even though it may not have been the best situation for them—and I'm really in no place to judge that—this father's desire for connection with his son was a good thing.

And then there's my friend Brian. Brian used to be an intern at XXXchurch, but before then he was just a high school kid struggling with porn. He found out about x3Watch and installed it on his home computer, setting up his youth pastor as his accountability partner, the person who would receive the reports.

One day Brian's youth pastor called him and said, "Hey, Brian, I just got your report and saw some of the sites you've been looking at. Wanna talk about it?"

This took Brian by surprise. Not because he'd been caught in the act, but specifically for the opposite reason—he hadn't done a thing.

Fortunately, their relationship was deep enough and strong enough and they'd built up enough trust that Brian's youth pastor believed him when he denied being the one responsible for the activity. They talked for a little while to figure out the mystery and determined that it had to have been Brian's brother, using Brian's computer. So the pair of them went to Brian's brother to confront him.

Except he didn't do it either.

So now they were really baffled. They started to chalk it up to a glitch in the software when one of them noticed the time stamp on the report. See, x3Watch gives a detailed report of not just the sites you visit but the date and time you visit them. Looking over the times, it all fell into place.

The report indicated that Brian's computer had been used to access porn while Brian and his brother were at school. And that left one other person.

Their dad.

Can you appreciate Brian's situation at this point? He was a high school student trying to do the right thing, and now he'd just found out that his own father was using his computer to look at porn. And Brian knew it was going to be up to him to confront his dad about it.

How do you even go about doing that?

In Brian's case, he just bit the bullet and did it. One morning before school Brian went to his dad, the report in hand, and told him about x3Watch, what it did, and that it was installed on his computer. He showed his dad the report, the time stamps, and the sites that were visited.

You know what Brian's dad did? He denied it!

But only for a few hours. Because later that day Brian's dad called him and came clean. And what started as an awkward confrontation between a high schooler and his dad became a healthy, deep conversation about each of their struggles and the need for accountability.

In the end, Brian's dad began seeking accountability (with Brian and another man who was more of a peer), and the two of them were able to deepen their relationship and create yet another layer of accountability for Brian.

Just like bad things can happen when you loop family members into the accountability circle (like my friend "Joseph" and his credit-card-wielding wife), so can good things (like with Adam and his wife, Michelle; the "Porn and Pancakes" dad and son; or Brian and his dad).

Ultimately, it's up to you to determine which of your family—if any—will walk down the road of accountability with you. And if you have a family member or spouse who is seeking accountability, don't pressure them to include you in their group. Let that come organically. If they want you in, they'll ask you. And if not, you don't want to force your way in. All you'll succeed in doing then is creating an environment of insecurity.

Family in My Group

As for my own accountability group, it is made up entirely of friends, and that is by design. While my wife is a great helper and my best friend, she also understands that there are things I need to discuss in that group that make more sense there than they do in our marriage relationship. I don't hold back anything from her, but I also don't share anything that the other guys in the group are going through, trusting that they're doing the same thing with their own spouses.

As for the access I give my wife, it can only be described as "full." We not only tell each other everything, but she gets my x3Watch reports (and I get hers), and we each have the other's passwords and log-in info for things like e-mail, Twitter, and Facebook. This is not so we can snoop into each other's private life or because we walk around full of suspicion. Quite the opposite. It's so we can live lives completely free of secrets, completely open to scrutiny. It's our way of saying to each other, "I have nothing to hide; I am an open book and completely welcome you into my world."

When I married my wife, I took a vow that I would walk

down the road of life with her by my side, and she took the same vow. We're not there to act as each other's authority figure—we got into this because we wanted to share our lives together and create something bigger between the two of us than either of us could've built on our own. We are in this to help each other, to support each other, and to take care of each other.

It's not my only accountability relationship, but it is the ultimate in deep accountability relationships, and it works for us.

Chapter 10

GET EFFECTIVE

*H*opefully by now you've decided you need to get accountable and that you also have the perfect person or two or three in mind to be your accountability partners—keeping in mind that these are people who also want to stay accountable—and now you're thinking, *So what do we do?*

Good question.

With this final chapter, let's answer it.

Schedule a Regular Meeting

One of the things that really makes accountability work is regularity. It's much more difficult to make bad choices when you know for a fact that you're going to be held to account on a certain day and at a certain time. The simple foundation of a regular schedule goes a long, long way toward influencing your—and your partners'—decisions for the better.

So, with that in mind, schedule a regular meeting that you know you'll each attend. Every time. It may be a little tough to find a time that works for everyone, but it's well worth making the plan and then following through on it. You'll probably only need about an hour, once a week. If you absolutely can't do once a week, you can try meeting every other week, but that sort of schedule lends itself to getting off-track and fizzling out. When you meet once a week, you have a much better chance of keeping that meeting.

Our accountability meeting time only lasts a half-hour, but we make the most of that half-hour, limiting small talk and hitting the ground running every week. And look, I know we're all busy in this world, but if these guys and I can find time in the midst of our hectic pace of life to meet for thirty minutes a week, I know you can.

Arrange a Meeting Place

Where should you meet? The only perfect answer is: wherever you want. If you want to meet in person—and there is a noticeable benefit to looking people in the eye and interpreting body language—then you can choose to meet at a central location like a coffee shop or bakery. Many people also like to meet in the mornings before work or school. The ease of slipping out of the house a little earlier than usual and getting your morning coffee to go with your accountability meeting is certainly an attraction.

Some people choose to meet for lunch once a week at a certain restaurant, or to pick a different restaurant every week to add a little variety to the proceedings. Like I said earlier, it's up to you.

There's no rule that says you must meet in a neutral location either. You can meet at someone's house or in a back room at your church—I don't care if you meet in a refrigerated boxcar that's hauling frozen fish sticks to your nearest retailer (as long as you dress appropriately). All I care about is that you agree on a place and follow through.

Technology has opened up the possibilities in multiple ways now too. Our group meets through a conference call, but we could just as easily use Skype, Google Plus, iChat AV, or some other form of video chat program over the Internet. I suppose if you had to, even a text-based instant messenger (like iChat or even Facebook chat) could do the trick, though that lends itself to distraction and misinterpretation. If I can't be in the room with someone, I like to at least be able to hear their voice to get tonal cues and things of that nature.

One more thing: if you choose to meet in person at a physical location, make sure you choose a place where you'll all feel comfortable airing out the best and worst in yourselves, and where sensitive ears won't be around to listen to you. If you're working on your compulsion to frequent strip clubs, you may want to think twice before you meet at the park during a play-date with the kids. In a lot of ways, a busy restaurant or coffee shop is actually conducive to helping you unburden yourself—the constant hum of background noise from the other patrons and their conversations can act as a kind of safety blanket, providing a music bed of sorts upon which you can lay out your thoughts. If you're meeting in a deathly quiet back room, suddenly your words sound a lot more ominous; you may wind up not uttering them, fearing their weight.

Decide a Format

You have your meeting time and place picked out, so now all you have to do is actually meet with your accountability partner or group. But what does that look like? What do you even do at a meeting? If you don't go into it with a plan, you'll probably wind up making a lot of small talk about one another's family or about the results of last night's game, or recapping the funniest lines from the sitcom you watched the previous evening. Then, when it's almost time to go, you'll look at one another awkwardly, mumble a little bit about the struggles you had last week, and then say your good-byes and go about your day.

In case you haven't guessed it by now, that is not what we're looking for here.

Honesty can be spontaneous, but spontaneity often arises from planning. I know that sounds like an oxymoron or some sort of holistic guru mumbo jumbo, but it's true. Lay down some framework with some ground rules and you build a nice skeleton upon which you can hang some serious honesty.

So with that in mind, I recommend a meeting format that goes something like this:

- Small talk and chitchat, but only for five minutes or so at the most—try to hit the ground running
- For people of faith, an opening prayer
- A series of staple questions you each ask to the others (more on those in a moment)
- Any specific question(s) that apply directly to you
- Again, for people of faith, a closing prayer
- Any further discussion you may want to have, be it more small talk or maybe a deeper conversation provoked by the meeting you just had
- Dismiss

It really is as simple as that. You can see that this barebones format allows for a lot of range in how the meeting goes.

Ask Questions

Now, about those questions. Obviously, this is your meeting with your accountability group, so you and your accountability partners can ask whatever questions you feel are necessary or helpful or beneficial. But so that you don't have to write all those questions from scratch, here are some ideas for questions you can ask one another:

- How was your week?
- Did the things you said and did this week make your life better? Did they represent you well to the rest of the world?
- How have you treated those who are important to you this week? Did you honor them and treat them with grace and generosity?
- Did you use any of your words as weapons this week, either to someone's face or behind their backs?
- What about anger? Are you angry or resentful toward someone? Are you holding on to that anger or letting it go?
- What about your stuff? Have you been trustworthy with your money and belongings this week?
- Have you indulged in lusts or anything of a sexual nature, whether physically or mentally?
- Have you caved in to any of your addictions or weaknesses this week?
- Were you honest and truthful in all you did?
- Did you take at least one full day off from work this week?
- If you were triggered, and this trigger was new, how can you avoid this next time?
- State one lie you have told someone in the past week or a secret you are keeping from someone else or the group.

- In one or two words, state how you are feeling emotionally right now.
- Did you lie to me in your answers to any of these questions?

Like I said, these are just a start—by all means feel free to modify these as needed to match the struggles within your own group. These are meant to be conversation starters, and if you don't see these as starting the particular conversation you need to have, then come up with your own questions. You can use these as a guide to do just that.

If you've been following along through the previous chapters about my own journey within my current accountability group, you'll know that we have a short list of questions that we each answer the night before our meeting and then e-mail to one another so that we already know the answers when we begin our conference call. Most of the questions I listed above are not on our list—ours is really very simple and consists of about four or five questions (depending on the individual). The idea is to get to the point quickly and leave as much room for talking as we need.

But while we have a few general questions that we all answer, we also have one or two very specific questions that pertain only to us personally, addressing a specific thing that we're working on. How might this work in your group? Here's an example.

Let's say one of you is trying to quit smoking; the obvious question for that person would then be, "Did you use any tobacco this week?" (You could ask, "Did you smoke a cigarette?" but then what if they smoked a pipe? Or "Did you smoke?" would work, unless they'd taken up chewing tobacco. You get the idea.) But if another of you is trying to manage his schedule better, then you could ask him a question like, "Did you use your time wisely and productively, or were you wasteful?"

Take the time to make these questions work for you, and especially keep in mind the truth we discussed earlier: some questions will stay on the list for the rest of your life, while others will fall off and get replaced with new ones. That's awesome! It's a sign of progress.

Go Beyond the Weekly Meeting

The weekly meeting is a great thing, and it's well worth it to seek out that time together, face-to-face (if you can), one-on-one. That interaction is crucial. But if that's the only time each week you're talking to your accountability partner or other members of your group, then you're doing it wrong.

These should be people you're intentionally welcoming into your life, and that means embracing their presence on more than just a frequency of a half-hour once a week. I'm not suggesting you need to have them over for dinner every night or to head over to their backyard for a barbecue and some quality time on their trampoline. I am saying that this relationship needs to extend past your usual meeting.

How so? For starters, as I said before, our group has a

written caveat that you have to connect with at least one other person in the group during the week, whether that's a phone call or e-mail or lunch or personal visit to their home. That's a nonnegotiable part of our group. Additionally, I have other friends whom I've given the liberty to call or text me at any time of the day or night, just to check in and see how I'm doing or to tell me they are in a tempting spot and are leaning toward making a bad decision. And I have the right to do the same thing.

Almost all phones seem to be smart these days; set a reminder in your phone to connect with your accountability partners a couple of other times during the week, just to see what happens. As I write this, there are almost more ways to keep in touch than I can list: phone, text, e-mail, instant message, Facebook, Twitter, Tumblr, Instagram . . . I'm almost afraid to list them because I don't want this list to be outdated in a couple of years. The point being: you have no excuse for not at least trying to stay connected with your accountability partners throughout the week.

Now, if they don't contact you back, then it might be time to take it to the next level and search them out in person. This happens more than you might think. As soon as we start trying to work on our junk, we seem to make ourselves suddenly more susceptible to falling prey to it, often out of shame or feelings of despair or self-pity. Don't let this happen to your accountability partners! If they aren't responding to you, the chances are good there's a reason, and that reason is often going to be because they're off making bad choices.

Or maybe you're the one making bad choices. Maybe you

are having a tough time and are falling back into some old, unhelpful, unhealthy patterns. That's okay. Just stay in touch, and things will get better. I promise.

Going Dark

Speaking of staying in touch, one of the worst pitfalls in an accountability relationship I've ever seen is the phenomenon my friend Jared calls "going dark." Jared has had his share of struggles in his life, and as a result he has taken on several different accountability partners—instead of a group of four or five people, he meets one-on-one with a handful of different people to keep himself as honest as possible (he refers to himself as "an accountability polygamist").

One of those accountability partners is a guy we'll call "Seth." Seth is a friend of his from college who battles a severe addiction to sex: not just using porn but also going to strip clubs, hiring prostitutes, and other such matters. Seth was actively working on doing the difficult job of letting go of this behavior, and part of his growth was in partnering up with Jared for some accountability.

They were meeting very regularly and had even started talking on the phone every day, just to check in with each other to see how everything was going with their separate struggles.

Then one day Seth stopped calling.

And he wouldn't answer when Jared called.

Days went by. Then weeks.

Nothing.

That's going dark.

Instead of upholding his side of the accountability bargain, Seth did his best to disappear into thin air. Fortunately, however, Jared wasn't going to let Seth go out like that. So Jared continued trying to reach Seth and essentially became the squeaky wheel in Seth's life. Calling him, e-mailing him, dropping by his house . . . Jared did everything he could to find Seth and find out what was up.

After a week of constant persistence, Jared tracked down Seth and asked him why he went dark.

"No reason," Seth responded. "Everything's fine."

Jared pushed for a better, more thorough answer, knowing that people don't go dark when "everything's fine." Seth was adamant that things were going great, and that was all the information he would offer. Jared did his best, told Seth he was on his side and in his corner, and hung up.

A week went by, and Jared made contact with Seth once more, and this time he got the full truth: Seth had cheated on his wife with a prostitute and was now getting kicked out of his house and was headed for a separation.

I wish that story had a happier ending, but as I write this, Seth is still separated from his wife, and Jared doesn't know how it's going to turn out. I asked Jared for some thoughts on going dark, and he said, "It's gut-wrenching to see your friends destroy their lives before your eyes."

Jared has hit on a core truth that I cannot emphasize enough, especially when we're talking about when your accountability partner goes dark: you are not responsible for their behavior. You cannot control them, and you shouldn't try. You love that person through thick and thin, but you let them make their own choices and live with the consequences of those choices. It can be incredibly difficult, especially for someone like Jared, who is watching a close friend throw his marriage into a garbage disposal in search of cheap pleasure, but Jared's job is not to throw a chastity belt on Seth; instead, it is to encourage him to change for the better and to live life with positivity in mind.

Nowadays, when Jared calls Seth, he's hoping to get an answer. The last time he talked to Seth, Jared told him, "I'm glad you answered the phone. That shows you're still wanting to get sober."

Seth's response really cuts to the core of accountability: "Honestly, I just appreciate your friendship."

When we talk about accountability, we're ultimately talking about friendship, about the kind of commitment and connection that goes the extra mile and that chases a friend into the dark when they try to go there, and at least says, "I'm here for you if you want to come out of this darkness." You can't make their decisions for them, but you can be a role model and lead them out of darkness by example.

Accountability Raids

Remember way back in an earlier chapter when I talked about my friend and former NFL quarterback Jon Kitna? Remember his group that is so strong they call themselves a "covenant group"? Well, they have an intriguing thing they do that they refer to as an "accountability raid."

Basically, if any two or more of the members of this covenant group are together, one of them can yell out, "Accountability raid!" and everyone has to give their phone to another member of the group. That member then can scroll through the phone's Internet browser history, text messages, photos, and any other social media apps (like the offline, direct-message features of Twitter or Facebook) to see if the phone's user has been on the up-and-up. This would also apply to any computers in the room or any other piece of technology that might provide a means of slipping up in their commitments to one another.

Maybe that sounds a little extreme to you, but I love it. I mean, do you want true accountability or not? Do you want to live a fuller, richer, deeper, more successful life, unhindered by the garbage of temptation, or don't you? Maybe something like these accountability raids aren't your cup of tea, or maybe they make you uncomfortable because you know you might wind up failing one.

Once more, accountability requires total honesty and courage, and the concept of the accountability raid simply takes those attributes to their next logical level. The accountability raid provides you with an opportunity to be honest and courageous outside your normal accountability time.

Now, just to make sure we're being totally clear here, the accountability raid is a rarity even among Jon's covenant group. It's not like they do it every time they sit down with one another. Some of the members of the group haven't even been subjected to an accountability raid yet.

But knowing that the possibility of an accountability raid is out there has helped some of the members of this covenant group as they strive to become the best versions of themselves they can be. Something to consider when you're putting together your own group (or joining one that is being put together by someone else).

What to Do if It Isn't Working

Don't expect everything to go great right from the start of your first accountability meeting. You and your accountability partners will need to make course corrections along the way, seeking out and discovering which methodologies and formats fit you best. Maybe you'll take awhile settling on a particular venue, or maybe you'll need to revisit your meeting time and switch from mornings to late nights. Maybe you'll find that the questions you originally thought would be great are just ho-hum and aren't really cutting to the heart of the matter.

Change things! If it isn't working, change it.

And speaking of change, there is one particular change that becomes sort of the nuclear option in accountability, the big change you make only when you are clear that no one is benefiting from this relationship, and that change is letting loose of either your group or someone in your group or, if you're meeting just with one other person, your accountability partner in general.

The sad thing is that some people only see meeting with an accountability partner as a way to lecture someone or to put them down or to make them feel bad so they feel good, or just because they're a nosy busybody who wants to get into someone else's business. These things happen. Hopefully you've been able to recognize those types of people and screen them out before you ever took the accountability leap with them in the first place, but if you're stuck with a dud, please know that you are not stuck with them.

Remember, I'm the supposed accountability expert, the guy who is writing an entire book on the subject, and yet my main accountability group has only half the people we started with. Why? Because for those other guys, it just wasn't working.

Like I said: if it isn't working, change it.

How will you know it isn't working? You'll know. You want to come away from your accountability meetings challenged and encouraged. Some of the stuff you're walking through may be tough, but while you're in the valley, you at least know you have a friend by your side who won't leave you in there to fend for yourself. I'm not saying you'll leave every meeting time ecstatic and happy—on the contrary, I can guarantee you won't. You'll have a time or two or ten where you may even feel beaten down and defeated.

But as long as you know you have that person or group of people by your side, then no matter how bad it gets, you know deep down inside you'll make it through. If you don't have that feeling—if, instead, you feel despondent and depressed, like the person you're meeting with is exacerbating your problems or making your life worse in general—then start to take a long, hard look at the relationship and try to determine if it's irreparably damaged. It may be that you're just not a good fit for each other.

And, finally, you'll know it isn't working if your account-ability group is not seasoning every interaction with grace and unselfishness. I cannot stress this enough. This is not a competition to see who is the humblest, and it is not a time to put others down so you feel better about yourself. This is the ultimate test of graciousness and humility, both in talking and listening, and if you aren't seeing those things in the other people in your group or if you aren't personally bringing those things to the table every time, then it's time to reassess.

I want to stress these are the minority of cases when it comes to accountability. These times of having to walk away from an accountability relationship are so rare that I hesitate even to talk about it. But I know it's inevitably going to happen to someone somewhere, so it needed to be addressed.

The chances are far greater that you won't even need this section of the book. So if you don't, great! And if you do, now you know how to move forward.

A FINAL WORD

I wish this one was a football story, but I will have to go with baseball on this one. There is no better word to describe the baseball player Sandy Koufax than *legend*. He was already a pitching great when he took the mound for the Los Angeles Dodgers on a cool September evening in 1965, ready to square off against the Chicago Cubs, though he hadn't been pitching particularly well in the weeks leading up to this game.

Still, he stepped up, took the ball, and proceeded to make history.

The thing about Koufax is that, according to his biographer Jane Leavy, he had a bad habit of spoiling the secrets of his pitches with his body language. Opposing batters could examine his windup and, based on how many "hitches" he had, tell whether he was about to throw a fastball or a curveball.

Yet, on that night, pitch after pitch after pitch, not a single batter for the Cubs could get a hit.

Oh, they made plenty of contact—a line drive here, a fly ball there. But none of those balls ever made it into the field of play, thanks to the fine fielding skills of the rest of the Dodgers. Cubs catcher Chris Krug made some waves in the sixth inning, hitting a tricky grounder to Dodgers shortstop Maury Wills, who fielded and turned it over to Wes Parker at first base. Wills's throw was low and in the dirt, but Parker got to it and Krug was out.

The next batter was Cubs shortstop Don Kessinger, who again made contact and sent a dribbler down the third-base line. Fortunately, Dodgers third baseman Junior Gilliam had been expecting a bunt and was close enough to nab the ball and just barely throw out Kessinger at first.

And so it went, batter after batter, inning after inning, until finally Harvey Kuenn struck out to end the game and preserve a perfect game for Sandy Koufax: he retired twenty-seven straight batters, allowing none of them to reach base.

Koufax gets the accolades for this historic game—sometimes called the greatest game ever pitched—and eventually his career exploits would make him the youngest person ever elected to the Baseball Hall of Fame.

But he didn't get there by himself.

He relied on people like Wills and Parker, like Gilliam and catcher Jeff Torborg.

The fact of the matter is, you can't have a perfect game without getting picked up by the rest of the team.

Do you know how rare the perfect game is? According to MLB.com, there have only been twenty-three perfect games in the history of Major League Baseball.[1] Twenty-three! Over the course of a season, every team plays at least 162 games. There are thirty teams in Major League Baseball, so now you do the math. Okay, I'll do it for you: that makes 4,860 games pitched every year. And now we're looking at the past almost century and a half of baseball and finding that there have only been twenty-three perfect games.

That's how amazing Koufax's feat was. And it's an amazing thing that can happen to you, when you stop relying on yourself and start allowing others into your life to back you up, to pick you up, to dust you off, to help you keep going when all seems lost.

Look, we're all big bags of screwups and mistakes. Not one of us has led a perfect life, so we need to have grace for one another as we interact. Every single one of us has something we need to work on, some habit or behavior we could stand to let go.

Life is a record of letting things go.

We all have to pick one another up—that's the nature of accountability. That's the thing that counts. At some point, it'll be our turn to take the mound, and we want to know we can count on everyone in the infield to pick us up, to turn the occasional double play, to field the grounders and fly balls.

Because when we do, we all win.

And sometimes you're going to have a less-than-perfect game. Even legends lose now and then—Koufax went on to lose to the Cubs five days later—but it doesn't spoil their achievements.

You can do this. You must do this.

A life of freedom, confidence, and security is waiting for you. It's there for the having.

What will you do?

PUTTING YOUR GROUP TOGETHER

*H*opefully by this point you now realize your need for accountability. And perhaps you are thinking of people who can be in your accountability group. Perhaps your brain is buzzing, your mind is swimming with all the whens and wheres and whos that something like accountability requires of you.

But maybe you don't know where to begin. Maybe you're now completely overwhelmed by all that must be done, and you don't have anyone in your life you can get accountable with.

Before you take out a "looking for accountability partner" ad on Craigslist, let's look at some possible resources for you.

Foundational Tenets of Accountability Groups

For starters, your group, whether it is one-on-one or includes several people, must be a supportive and safe environment, where anything can be said and accepted, whether or not it is acceptable.

Your group must be honest and courageous, a place where you can have authentic conversations with no pretense or fakery.

Every word, action, hand gesture, and facial expression must be filled with grace, with no room for judgment or condemnation.

It is a good idea to share your accountability group with others who have similar struggles and stories, but maybe not the exact same story as you.

Each of you must have the mind-set that you can and will learn something from the other person or people in your group. This is not a place for you to get on a soapbox or try to fix everyone else's problems.

And finally, something that especially applies to those who start out on accountability as a result of an encounter with XXXchurch, the accountability group environment must be one where everyone has an opportunity to process their thoughts and feelings verbally, especially as they pertain to sexual triggers and remedy actions. This is not a place where someone has to think through what they're going to say in order to avoid offense—if you need to process something out loud, whether to yourself or to another person, you should have the right and freedom to do so, just as they should feel those same rights and freedoms themselves.

Okay, now that we've established the foundational tenets of your group, let's go deeper.

Confronting the Fears

What if you are seeking accountability for some sort of life-derailing behavior, like chemical or alcohol dependency, or some other addiction (like gambling or sex or porn or the like)? Your recovery depends on accountability. Unfortunately, at XXXchurch, we've found that many people often have difficulty once they try to find a suitable accountability source. What holds them back?

For starters, many people have to overcome their fear of being found out. Remember how we talked about that fear and how accountability can bring the freedom you need from that hollow stomach feeling, the dread of being discovered? That can be a tough thing to give up, because it's one thing to admit you have a problem but it is quite altogether another thing entirely to trust someone else with that information. Instead, it's easy and convenient to perceive your isolation as something it isn't: safety. It's terribly simple to convince your-self that accountability will only bring condemnation and rejection at the hands of someone else, and therefore decide to skip accountability altogether. This is a major hurdle, and for some it's a deal breaker. If that's the case for you, then I can't do anything about that other than to encourage you to give it a try and see what happens. The alternative is to keep going down the same road you've been on, and you already know that's taking you nowhere.

Once you clear that hurdle of actually opening up to being accountable, the next difficulty you'll probably encounter lies in asking the right person or people to help keep you account-able. Remember, you must find someone who will treat you honestly and respectfully but who will not buy any excuses or let you off the hook with well-meant encouragement when you experience failure and compromise. And when we're talking about life-derailing behaviors like sexual addiction or drug and alcohol dependence, there is an extremely high likelihood that you will experience failure and compromise.

But then you also don't want to deal with the opposite problem of finding an accountability source who only wants to preach at you, lecture you, call you on the carpet, and treat you like you're a renegade cop who needs to have your badge and gun taken away and be thrown off the force. You don't want to be paired up with someone who will condemn you and, even worse, never encourage or love you.

So what to do?

At XXXchurch, we often receive e-mails from both men

and women who are valiantly and relentlessly struggling with sexual addiction or lust issues, people who are crying out to us and asking us where they can go for accountability and support. The task is made even more difficult because, in our arena, the subject of sex—or rather of wayward sexual impulses or lust—is seen as so taboo as to be completely avoided, causing many people and churches to blindly ignore the issue. Holding someone accountable for his or her sexual misconduct can be uncomfortable and invasive, so these churches or people—wrongfully—instead feel it's better to pretend it doesn't even exist.

Additionally, many people find it hard to relate to people who struggle with certain types of behaviors if they have no frame of reference for such behaviors in themselves. If they've never battled a serious addiction to alcohol, drugs, gambling, sex, or any of the other myriad things we can become addicted to, then they'll naturally have an uphill battle at putting themselves in the mind-set of someone who does.

RESOURCES FOR ACCOUNTABILITY

X3 GROUPS ARE CHRIST CENTERED SUPPORT GROUPS FOR THOSE STRUGGLING WITH SEXUAL ADDICTION. LOCAL LIVE GROUPS ARE AVAILABLE MEETING FACE-TO-FACE THROUGHOUT THE COUNTRY.

X3GROUPS.COM

TO WRITE LOVE ON HER ARMS IS A NON-PROFIT MOVEMENT DEDICATED TO PRESENTING HOPE AND FINDING HELP FOR PEOPLE STRUGGLING WITH DEPRESSION, ADDICTION, SELF-INJURY, AND SUICIDE. TWLOHA EXISTS TO ENCOURAGE, INFORM, INSPIRE, AND ALSO TO INVEST DIRECTLY INTO TREATMENT AND RECOVERY.

THE VISION IS HOPE, AND HOPE IS REAL.

VISIT TWOLHA.COM FOR MORE

Other Resources

Here are a few additional resources to help you in other areas where you may have struggles. These are all places and organizations where you can learn foundational principles to overcome whatever obstacles you may have in your way, while also complementing those principles with a strong core of accountability.

- Financial Peace University: This is a program available through financial guru Dave Ramsey that focuses on helping people gain control of their finances. You can find out more online at DaveRamsey.com/FPU.
- Jenny Craig: This organization offers weight-loss programs and products along with different ideas and tips for cooking healthier and living a more robust lifestyle. There is more information about this program available online at JennyCraig.com.
- Weight Watchers: This is another weight-loss program, though with more emphasis on group accountability and meetings. Information is available at WeightWatchers.com.
- CrossFit: This is an intense exercise program geared at creating general physical fitness and achieving results across the spectrum of physical exertion. It is very focused on camaraderie and accountability. Daily workouts and other information are posted at CrossFit.com.
- Heart Support: Heart Support is a nonprofit organization built on a foundation of faith; it desires to

strengthen the youth of today. An online community built to encourage, inspire, and bring a message of hope, It is a place for the youth to talk about struggles and difficult issues and to find healing and strength in this community. www.heartsupport.com.

- Alcoholics Anonymous: A twelve-step program for those struggling with an addiction to alcohol. For more information or to find a meeting in your area, visit their official website at AA.org.
- Sexaholics Anonymous: Similar to AA, but for those struggling with sexual addiction. For more information or to find a meeting in your area, visit their official website at SA.org.
- Gamblers Anonymous: Similar to AA and SA, but for those struggling with an addiction to gambling. More information about support groups—and an online test to determine your level of addiction— is available through their official website, GamblersAnonymous.org.
- Celebrate Recovery: A holistic approach to recovery for anyone struggling with hurts, habits, and hang-ups. Further information about the program and meeting times and locations can be found online at their official website, CelebrateRecovery.com.
- Waypost: An app for your mobile phone that takes accountability to the next level, Waypost allows your accountability partner (or whomever you choose) the opportunity to check your physical location based on

the GPS in your smartphone. Great for spouses to keep tabs on each other or for parents to know where their kids are and where they're headed. You can find out more info, sign up, or download the app at Waypost.net.

- eMeals: eMeals is the simple dinner solution for busy people who want to spend their money wisely and their time with people they love. eMeals is the easy way to be organized, have a well-managed grocery budget and enjoy healthy dinners at home. See www.emeals.com.

ACKNOWLEDGMENTS

*T*hanks to Adam Palmer for writing with me on this book and all the others. Thanks to Esther Fedorkevich for believing in this project and the work that I do. The whole team at Thomas Nelson has been amazing to work with, but thanks especially to Joel Miller for saying yes to this book. Jon Kitna and Eric Boles, thank you for your honesty and transparencies with your "covenant group," which inspired me to try and duplicate it. Tom Ramsey and Jake Larson, thanks for those early-morning McDonald's meetings that served as the foundation for all of this. Ryan Russell, thanks for letting me steal some of your stories and, more importantly, for your friendship. All of the Fireproof Ministries staff and volunteers, you inspire me. Thanks, Mom, for everything you have done for me. Nolan, Elise, and Jeanette, I hope I make you proud, not by what I write but by how I try and live this stuff out.

—Craig

Thanks to Thomas Nelson for agreeing with us that this book needs to exist. Thanks to Craig for roping me in then pushing me to make this thing better and better and better. Thanks to Chris, Robert, Sean, Eric, and Paul for being guys I can count on. Thanks to Michelle and the kids for understanding when I had to spend a few of our summer vacation days working, and also for being—in all ways, shapes, and forms—awesome. Thanks to Jesus for everything.

—Adam

NOTES

Chapter 1: Accountability Is Good

1. Nicholas Carlson, "How Many Users Does Twitter REALLY Have?" *Business Insider*, March 21, 2011. Available at http://articles.businessinsider.com/2011-03-31/tech/30049251_1_twitter-accounts-active-twitter-user-simple-answer.
2. To download the free x3Watch software or a free fifteen-day trial of x3Watch Pro, go to http://www.x3watch.com/x3watchfree.html.
3. Kesavan Unnikrishnan, "Study: Facebook Cited in a Third of Divorces in 2011," *Digital Journal*, January 1, 2012. Available at http://digitaljournal.com/article/317055.

Chapter 2: Accountability Is Safety

1. Fox News Insider, "Secret Service Agents Dismissed in Prostitution Scandal; President Obama Calls Them

'Knuckleheads' on Late Night with Jimmy Fallon," April 4, 2012. Available at http://foxnewsinsider.com/2012/04/24/secret-service -agents-dismissed-in-prostitution-scandal-president-obama-calls -them-knuckleheads-on-late-night-with-jimmy-fallon/.

2. Fox News Insider, "Secret Service Outlines Specific Guidelines for Agents in Wake of Prostitution Scandal," April 28, 2012. Available at http://foxnewsinsider.com/2012/04/28/secret-service-outlines -specific-guidelines-for-agents-in-wake-of-prostitution-scandal/.

3. Jeff Bullas, "48 Significant Social Media Facts, Figures and Statistics Plus 7 Infographics," *Business to Community*, April 23, 2012. Available at http://www.business2community.com /social-media/48-significant-social-media-facts-figures-and -statistics-plus-7-infographics-0167573.

Chapter 3: Accountability Is Deep

1. *Raising Arizona*, screenplay by Ethan Coen and Joel Coen, 1987. Available at http://www.imsdb.com/scripts/Raising-Arizona.html.

Chapter 4: Accountability Is Necessary

1. Hank Haney, *The Big Miss: My Years Coaching Tiger Woods* (New York: Crown Publishing Group, 2012).

2. "Tiger Woods' Apology: Full Transcript," CNN.com, February 29, 2010. Available at http://www.cnn.com/2010/US/02/19/tiger .woods.transcript/index.html.

Chapter 5: You Need Honesty

1. Ryan Russell, "'Yes Men' Are Posers," RedBikeLeader.com, August 4, 2011. Available at http://www.redbikeleader.com/2011 /yes-men-are-posers/.

Chapter 6: You Need Courage

1. Kevin Johnson and Erin Egan, "Report Slams Penn State's 'Total Disregard' in Sandusky Case," USAToday.com, July 12, 2012. Available at http://www.usatoday.com/news/nation/story

/2012-07-11/penn-state-investigation-sandusky/56162986
/1?csp=34news. Quoting from Freeh Sporkin & Sullivan, LLP,
"Report of the Special Investigative Counsel Regarding the
Actions of the Pennsylvania State University Related to the Child
Sexual Abuse Committed by Gerald A. Sandusky," July 12, 2012.
Available at http://www.cbsnews.com/htdocs/pdf/2012/REPORT
_FINAL_071212.pdf.
2. Ibid.
3. Ibid.

Chapter 8: Get Involved

1. Ryan Russell, "Motivation Comes from Achieving the Next Level,"
RedBikeLeader.com, October 28, 2010. Available at http://www.
redbikeleader.com/2010/the-next-level/.
2. Jonah Lehrer, "Why Smart People Are Stupid," *New Yorker*, June
12, 2012. Available at www.newyorker.com/online/blogs
/frontal-cortex/2012/06/daniel-kahneman-bias-studies.html.
3. Ibid.

A Final Word

1. MLB.com, "Rare and Memorable Feats: Perfect Games."
Available at http://mlb.mlb.com/mlb/history/rare_feats/index
.jsp?feature=perfect_game.

ABOUT THE AUTHORS

Craig Gross

Craig Gross is an author, speaker, pastor, and revolutionary. He shot to prominence in 2002 when he cofounded the website XXXchurch.com as a response to the hurting he saw both in those addicted to pornography and those who made their living in the porn industry. Craig also spearheaded the development of X3watch, an Internet accountability system that is used by over one million people.

Craig is the author of nine books and has been featured in *GQ*, *Newsweek*, *Wired*, the *New York Times*, and the *Los Angeles*

Times. He has also appeared on *Good Morning America*, *Nightline*, CNN, Fox News, and *The Daily Show with Jon Stewart*. He currently resides in Pasadena, California, with his wife, Jeanette, and their children, Nolan and Elise.

www.getopen.com
www.craiggross.com
www.twitter.com/craig_gross
www.facebook.com/craiggross

Adam Palmer

Adam Palmer is a hardworking freelance writer who has worked on over thirty books as a writer, cowriter, contributor, or editor, including all of the previous titles by Craig Gross. He has also written for stage and screen. He has been writing professionally since he was seventeen years old and hasn't looked back since. He currently lives in Tulsa, Oklahoma, with his wife and five children.

www.twitter.com/ThatAdamPalmer

INDEX